Co

Dedication

For their guidance and inspiration, thanks to my teachers, Arthur Little, Charles Bates, John Franklyn-Robbins, and Tom McNally.
For her friendship and soaring spirit, thanks to Linda Seka.
For her help in proofreading, thanks to my mother, June Stark.
For the love, humor, and excellence in our lives, thanks to my husband, Frank Dwyer.

The author is sensitive to the absence of a non-specific gender designator in English. Those temporary solutions occasionally used by enlightened writers are, at best, awkward. For the sake of style and ease in reading, the traditional masculine pronouns have been used in this book.

The author does not suggest the practice of any physical exercise without the consultation and supervision of one's personal physician. While the author stands behind the value, benefits, and advisability of the techniques and exercises described in this book, she does not guarantee the specific outcomes derived from their practice.

THE PROFESSIONAL ACT

Acting Communication Technique

Mary Stark

Metamorphous Press
Portland, Oregon

Published by

Metamorphous Press
P.O. Box 10616
Portland, Oregon 97210

Photos used with permission. Special thanks and appreciation to:
Alyce Cornyn-Selby, Beynch Press, for use of her photos;
Connie Connor, Just Communications, for modeling and photos;
George Green for photo services.

Editorial and Art Direction by Lori Stephens
Printed in the United States of America

Stark, Mary, 1952-
The professional A.C.T. : acting communication technique / Mary Stark.
p. cm.
Includes bibliographical references and index.
ISBN 1-55552-033-2 (pbk.)
1. Acting. 2. Public speaking. I. Title.
PN2061.S717 1992
792'.028—dc20 92-11595

Chapter 1

The Professional A.C.T.

I am an actress and I love performing on the stage, but public speaking used to be as terrifying for me as for most people who have no professional performing credits. The actor has the security of the memorized script which has been shaped and polished with the aid of a director over weeks of rehearsal. There is the illusion that the actor is transformed into another character who hides the actor's own identity, so even though exposed before an audience, the actor feels that his vulnerable core is protected from view.

I have many early memories of being called on to speak in church or assemblies and feeling flushed, struggling to keep my lower lip from trembling and my voice from quavering uncontrollably. It was only after many years as a professional actress that I resolved to confront my fear of public speaking and began a comprehensive study of public speaking techniques. The time had come to tackle this dreaded area of performance with the same commitment that I apply to my profession—my performances in the theater. I found that the techniques which I rely upon as an actress to sustain my energy, focus, and stamina on stage were easily adapted to public speaking and presentations. Learning how to "act" like a speaker has made me a much better speaker and communicator.

You too can learn acting techniques which will make you a more effective and successful speaker and communicator. Through a simple and disciplined course of study and by practicing the skills, you can become more expressive, more effective and persuasive in your communication and more successful in achieving your goals. In addition, you will learn to pick up non-verbal clues from other speakers which will reveal their true concerns and intentions and will give you an edge in judging how best to bring them around to your point of view. Finally, you will gain comfort and ease in communicating with groups of people as well as individuals. Your new confidence will further enhance your ability to convey information, give your opinions, and express your feelings. Learning to be a better communicator can influence every relationship, personal and professional, and improve every aspect of your life.

I've been a professional actress for seventeen years, working in theaters in Massachusetts, New York City, Pennsylvania, Illinois, and Indiana. I've performed my one-woman-show—*White Ashes: The Life and Writings of Harriet Beecher Stowe*—all over the country, with special engagements at the Smithsonian Institute and the Beecher family reunion in Hartford, Connecticut. I've worked in plays, musicals, television, films, industrial training videos, and commercials. I've been a professional director, and I've taught acting to people of all ages.

After several years of teaching a popular acting class on my nights off from the theater, I was asked if I would consider teaching a course for non-theater professional people—lawyers, doctors, teachers, salespeople, managers, and executives—who would benefit greatly if they could improve the way they speak and present themselves in public by learning the techniques of the professional actor and developing the acting skills that are latent in everyone. The success of my course—*The Professional A.C.T.: Acting Communication Technique*—has been so gratifying, with both careers and relationships enhanced, that I have decided to offer these techniques to a wider audience than can crowd a classroom.

What, first of all, do I mean by communication? For the speaker, communication is conveying information, which may

PHOTO COURTESY OF BEYNCH PRESS

Through a simple and disciplined course of study and by practicing the skills, you can become more expressive, more effective and persuasive in your communication, and more successful in achieving your goals.

be consciously encoded in words and gestures (the text), or unconsciously imparted by such things as tone, rhythm, energy, attitude and body language (the subtext). For the listener, communication is perceiving both what the speaker appears to be saying and what he is really saying—not always the same thing.

Good actors communicate just what they want to communicate—text and subtext—and they are expected to do it without any apparent effort. If the effort shows, it's probably because the actor is struggling with a difficult prop, tormented by a rebellious contact lens, or distracted by a doctor's beeper in the audience.

In reality, acting is 99% perspiration and 1% inspiration. The ease with which an actor executes the dialogue is the result of an enormous amount of work, both at home, thinking about the character, studying the play, and memorizing lines, and in the theater, rehearsing with the other actors and the director. All that preparation is backed up by years of training—of the voice, the body, and the psyche.

In fact, many actors feel terribly ill at ease when they don't know their lines, the blocking has not been set, and there have been no rehearsals--that is, whenever they are called on to speak spontaneously before a group of people or when they are being interviewed by the media. I don't know of any actor who hasn't suffered from the infamous "actor's nightmare": you dream you are in a play, you know your entrance cue is coming, but you cannot remember your lines! Or worse, you must either miss your entrance (unthinkable) or walk out naked!

It is a terrible feeling to be unprepared—naked, not knowing your lines--and it has happened to everyone—before a jury, in a classroom, at a board meeting, or with an important client. What saves actors (if they are not asleep!) is their long practice in dealing with "stagefright" and their ability to "use" the fear, to make even the physical sensations caused by anxiety and nervousness contribute to their performances. *The Professional A.C.T.* will teach you the techniques that actors use so that you can improve your ability to communicate and enhance your professional performance.

The same skills which allow an actor to perform with ease and grace can be learned by anyone who wants to enhance his ability to communicate, not only in speaking before large groups but also in important dialogues with individuals: employers, employees, co-workers, friends, spouses, children. *The Professional A.C.T.* is designed to help non-actors develop these valuable acting skills.

Have you ever tried to ask a question in a meeting or after a presentation and found that your normally melodious, commanding voice came out sounding breathy, quavering, or squeaky? Have you ever wondered if you could keep your knees from knocking until you finished your speech? Have you ever caught yourself making the same ineffectual gesture over and over again, or worse, felt that you had no idea what to do with your hands, which were stuck on the podium or hanging immobile down at your sides like weights? Yet perhaps at home, when you were rehearsing in front of the mirror, or while stir-frying vegetables for dinner, you were able to speak naturally, amusingly and with confidence.

The vocal and physical ease which actors possess onstage is not an accident of nature. It is cultivated through careful vocal and physical training, through specific exercises in speech, body awareness, and coordination that are practiced until they become "second nature." When facing situations that inspire fear, anxiety, or panic, the actor can confidently fall back on his training and speak and move with ease. Before going onstage, the actor can be poised and calm because he knows his "physical instrument" is prepared; his body itself will know what to do. Having warmed up physically and vocally beforehand, the

PHOTO COURTESY OF JUST COMMUNICATIONS

The same skills which allow an actor to perform with ease and grace can be learned by anyone who wants to enhance his ability to communicate, not only in speaking before large groups but also in important dialogues with individuals: employers, employees, co-workers, friends, spouses, children.

performer can concentrate on playing the role, on making the dramatic points and executing the actions of the character instead of being distracted by his fears and anxieties. He knows that his voice and body, disciplined by training, will not betray him.

Your self-confidence increases (and your anxieties diminish) when you learn to be at ease with your breath, voice and body, and when your material is well-prepared and well-rehearsed.

All of us have had the pleasure of hearing a speaker whose knowledge of the material and whose personal self-confidence and charisma were such that there was no need for notes or preparation. But for most people preparation and rehearsals are vital in order to feel confident about a public presentation. When you know your material backwards and forwards and feel committed to what you are saying, that's when the magic starts to happen. That's when you're able to relax enough so that inspiration can illuminate you and touch the minds and hearts of your audience. If you are worried about the words on the page to the extent that you can't make eye-contact with your audience, all they will get from you is words. This doesn't mean that you must memorize every word, although some speakers only feel confident if they can speak from memory, but you must know the material well enough so that your interest as a speaker is on your target, your audience, not your notes, your audio-visual aids, or yourself.

Alistair Cooke didn't use a teleprompter for his introductions for *Masterpiece Theatre.* He memorized his script but improvised little additions as they taped. In *The New Yorker*, October 12, 1992 in the "Talk of the Town," he says:

> It's an old-fashioned prescription, it is tougher on the memory and the nerves, but until I am conspicuously overwhelmed by Alzheimer's, I intend to stay with it and with the implied conviction that an emcee ought to be at all times a person thinking aloud about something which at the moment interests or absorbs him.

Mr. Cooke always gave the impression that we were invited guests in his study, and that he was sharing with us his insights about the selected piece of literature. Rather than lecturing at us, his style suggested that he was just talking to us.

Knowing that you are well-prepared, you eliminate the risk of losing your place in your notes. You will remember where on the page or notecard the next point is placed. You will then feel free to elaborate spontaneously if you feel the need, judging by the non-verbal audience cues. You will be confident about picking up where you left off in the prepared part of your presentation. You will know specifically how to lead up to the statement which will hook your audience, because you practiced the particular inflection which you require to make your point. You will feel secure about taking a pause after that particularly gripping argument in order to allow it to sink in on the audience. And your confidence in your subject will make your audience relax and be more receptive to what you say.

You have information which they want.

This book will teach you how to use your preparation and rehearsal time to your best advantage. You'll learn how to build a speech and how to break it down and orchestrate it so that it's interesting to listen to and expresses what you think and how you feel.

You will learn how to channel the wealth of energy at your disposal so that your communication becomes filled with vitality and reflects your personal style in a sincere and powerful way.

The speaker's purpose is to serve the audience or individual to whom he is communicating. Your sense of purpose focuses your attention away from your needs and makes you responsive to the needs of other people. You have information which they want. You have something to share which will persuade your listeners to your point of view because their needs will be met by your plan of action. At the time of your presentation, there is something which you want to share more than anything else which also should satisfy your audience's needs in some way.

You will learn the key to using a personal objective which dovetails with satisfying the needs of the people with whom you are communicating; this objective is fueled by energy which all of us have at our disposal but to which we may not have ready access. Many of you will discover that you need to "turn up the volume" of your energy and your intention in order to communicate more dynamically. You will learn to channel your mental and physical resources to fuel your needs as a public communicator in ways which will also enhance your interactions on a more personal level.

You will learn to trust yourself in unrehearsed situations when you need to rely on your intuition and spontaneity, and allow yourself the freedom to improvise creatively and effectively.

Have you ever walked into a situation feeling prepared only to find that you had to modify your strategy immediately or risk losing the attention and interest of a potential client? Robin Williams and Jonathan Winters are two experts at improvising spontaneously in front of an audience. They retain access to their imagination and their childlike ability to play in the moment. It's as if they turn off the critical voice inside, which, in many of us, makes us think twice before we say anything. That inner censor is a valuable advisor in many situations, but in a brainstorming session, it's those intuitive, uncensored ideas which often lead to creative solutions.

My first acting teacher used to say that if you're willing to be foolish, you won't appear foolish. It's the person who is walking so carefully, trying to be impressive and chic who invariably trips over his own feet and then tries to make it seem as if there was something in his way.

We will work to unlock those imaginative chambers which you may not have played in since you were a child. We'll dust out the cobwebs and make that space available for you as a resource for creative problem-solving.

You will learn how to listen to the non-verbal communication of others. We all use sub-textual cues in our body language and in our choice of communication channels. You'll become more adept in perceiving and interpreting those cues through the use of some Neurolinguistic techniques.

You'll become sensitized to the power you can assume just by standing still and using a few effective gestures rather than repeatedly touching your face or fiddling with your clothing. You'll recognize ways of developing rapport with another person by mirroring their posture, their inflections, and their methods of communication. When I return home to the Midwest, I find that I unconsciously assume the regional accent I have consciously tried to overcome in my professional work. It's like a chameleon changing in appearance to blend into the surroundings. Some people naturally focus on common traits or interests to give them an edge when it comes to breaking the ice with other people. Watch the really good interviewers on television like Bill Moyers or Oprah Winfrey. The rapport which they achieve seems effortless. You will learn how to make other people feel at ease and more receptive to your ideas without manipulating them.

Most people confess that their most debilitating fear is stagefright. You will learn procedures for working through stagefright and for developing an ability to relish the sense of aliveness which comes through performance and through meaningful experiences of communication with others.

Stagefright is an issue which fascinates me and which I learn more about with every performance. Even Laurence Olivier, late in his incredibly successful career, was paralyzed by stagefright. No one is immune, no matter how often they perform or present. It's important to recognize the symptoms for what they are. The exhilaration which I feel before performing is what fuels me, and the physical manifestations of that exhilaration include rapid heartbeat, shaking hands or knees, and hyperventilation. You will get to know through experience how your body functions in its "fight or flight" mode and move through those sensations with added fuel for your performance coming from the rush of adrenaline.

By committing yourself to the study of these acting, listening, and communication techniques, you are making an investment in your future as a professional in your chosen field. You have already mastered the specifics of your own area of expertise, and you have recognized that the ability to effectively communicate in public presentations will immeasurably enhance your chances to advance in your career. The second act of your professional life now begins with *The Professional A.C.T.*

Chapter 2 Body Language

The first and most powerful impression you give and receive is communicated through body language.

As a character actress, it is my business to interpret the character I am portraying by physically embodying that person. It is the highest compliment to me when I'm told by theater-goers that they didn't recognize me in a role. I don't do extensive character make-up, so whatever disguise I use is in my movement and voice. The body language which I arrive at is a combination of my imagination, the director's input, and the fine-tuning resulting from the feedback of the other actors and the audience. Actors know what force and immediate communication they can convey through body language. Non-theater people can use the same medium of expression to get their message across.

How do you know that this morning is a bad time to ask your supervisor for a raise, just by the way she walked past your desk? How do you know that your child or pet has destroyed something in the other room? How do people know that you have had a wonderful evening the night before, even though you are making an effort to be discrete?

We telegraph our emotions and our attitudes, in messages which are louder and clearer than any words, by the way we

> ***We telegraph our emotions and our attitudes, in messages which are louder and clearer than any words, by the way we walk, stand, sit, and make eye-contact.***

walk, stand, sit, and make eye-contact. If we are unconscious of the messages we are transmitting, we risk making an impression which may undermine our intentions. But if we are aware of the potential we have for making statements about ourselves through the use of our bodies, we can use body language to enhance and support our verbal communication.

In the first class of my *Professional A.C.T.* course, I ask students to write down their first impressions of everyone else, and then I ask them to notice if there are any discrepancies in the way they thought they presented themselves to others and the way others, in fact, perceived them. This is the first step in a process which we call recalibrating. "Know Thyself." We need to discover if we have a distorted sense of what is. That's why feedback is so important. We may think that we appear alert and receptive when other people may read us as diffident and sullen. So we need to practice working with our body, making an accurate assessment of how we present ourselves to others and then finding how to achieve the expression which we want to embody.

I have frown lines, and when I discovered that they were there even when I was feeling fine, I made a conscious decision to work to remove them. I smoothed them away, feeling what the sensation was when they were gone and what muscles I used (and didn't use) to try to maintain my smooth forehead. I had to find out how to make the physical adjustment in order to appear relaxed. Don't think that finding neutral is just a matter of relaxing. It takes effort to observe your body and make adjustments to counteract years of habit.

I have scoliosis, which is curvature of the spine. This condition means that I must make a lot of adjustments in order to be in alignment. In fact, I work really hard with an extensive exercise program and weights in order to strengthen muscles which have become atrophied because of lack of use and to relax muscles which have become overdeveloped to compensate. So I have a longer way to go than many people before I reach "neutral."

A teacher of mine told me a true story about a friend of his who was traveling to Africa to visit another man's ranch. The rancher could not meet him at the airport, so he sent a guide to pick up the traveler when he arrived. It was a long journey by car from the airport to the ranch, and the guide had other responsibilities which required his attention, so the plan was to take the traveler part way to where a Jeep was waiting, gassed up and ready for the traveler to drive himself the rest of the way to the ranch. The guide had a map, which he gave the traveler, which indicated the location of the ranch, and he made sure that the Jeep was in good running condition before he left. After the traveler had lingered long enough to enjoy the sunset, he got into the Jeep, started it, and looked at the map, only to find that his present location was not marked on the map! We sometimes are so concerned about our goal or destination that we forget that we need to know where we are in order to get where we want to go.

Before you attempt to do anything, you need to first come back to neutral, assessing where you are now. What messages are you getting from each part of your body, and how is your breath flowing? Eventually you will be able to do a quick inventory of your body and breath, focus your energy, and be ready to make your presentation or do your interview as quickly as you are reading these words now. You'll discover that the coming back to neutral process will make you more effective in your work and interpersonal relations so that this inventory will become a habit with you in any situation. But it takes practice, discipline and the desire to master these skills.

I've already talked about how the forehead is an indicator of stress or relaxation, surprise or serenity. The eyes are the mirrors of the soul. We can tell at a glance if someone is alert, hungover, hiding something from us, admiring us, impatient, cheerful, or raging just by looking at the eyes. Even a good actor would have difficulty maintaining an even gaze when confronted with an accusation of deceit. It's important to know that people want to look in your eyes when you're talking to them and when you're listening to them. Let your eyes be easy and relaxed, and let your gaze be direct without staring. If your eyes feel tired, a simple way to rest them and restore them to a more energized and expressive state is to lightly rub your hands together until they feel warm. Then bring the palms of your hands to your eyes, lightly cupping them over your eyes and holding them there for a few seconds. Know that when you lower your hands, your eyes will be brighter and will feel rested.

Recently, when a relative was visiting me I noticed that when she talked about herself, which was 95% of the time, she maintained steady eye-contact with me, but when she asked me about my work, she never looked at me. Consequently, I felt that she really didn't want to listen to me. I finessed the situation by allowing her to talk about what did interest her—herself.

When you are speaking to a group of people, allow yourself to make and maintain eye-contact with individuals in the audience. Don't just sweep back and forth mechanically—make connections with them as people. Look into their eyes and notice them. Don't stare. That will only make them uncomfortable, and you'll know because they will look away from you. People don't want to feel obligated to you by appearing to be enraptured with your every word, but they do want to feel that you are acknowledging them as real, flesh and blood people, not just an audience backdrop. If someone doesn't look at you, or has his eyes closed, don't take it personally. It doesn't matter. Talk to those who are looking at you and assume that the others are getting your message anyway.

The neck is the connecter between our head and heart. Consequently, there is often a lot of tension which gets stuck there. When my physical stamina is weakened, and I am most vulnerable to colds, I will feel the first symptoms in my throat. Likewise, if I am nervous or upset, my throat constricts, so it is difficult to speak. It feels as if someone's hand is gripping my throat, squeezing it to keep the sound from coming out. At these times, I experience the meaning of the words "to choke back emotions." The neck is the conduit between the head and the rest of the body. So when my heart is especially full of emotion, and I am unwilling or unable to find verbal expression for those emotions, I feel the blockage in my throat. It is as if an eight lane highway filled with traffic at rush hour is channeled into a single lane due to construction.

When the chin is locked down into the neck, it is physically protecting a vulnerable part of the body, the throat. Defensiveness, fear, or shyness is communicated. When a cat is relaxed and feels safe, it is willing to open this area up and let it be stroked. But if it feels threatened, the cat will pull back, protecting the throat from the possibility of attack.

On the other hand, when the head is thrown back, pinching the back of the neck, one communicates defiance. Those who hold their head with their nose in the air give the impression of haughtiness and false pride. Tilt the head to one side, and the effect is that you're interested or inquisitive.

The way your head is balanced over your body says a great deal about how you encounter the world. The Alexander Technique is a great method to practice which has an enormous impact on your general health and emotional well-being. I recommend my students to study and practice this technique. In the 1890's, F.M. Alexander, an actor living in Australia who recited Shakespeare in public, discovered that he was developing hoarseness and losing his voice. He began to methodically observe himself, using mirrors, attempting to detect the cause of his vocal problem. He found that whenever he began to speak, he habitually thrust his head down and back, which caused stress and tension on his larynx. He also noticed the pattern in other people, and he developed a

F. M. Alexander

method of teaching people a relationship between their head and spine which promoted health, relaxation, and a general sense of well-being. The benefits attributed to the practice of this technique include a lowering of blood pressure, the relief of tension headaches and low back pain, increased alertness during waking hours, deeper sleep at night, and even an enhancement of the ability to play musical instruments. The Alexander Technique is also reported to be successful in the treatment of peptic ulcers, spastic colons, ulcerated colitis, eczema, and rheumatoid arthritis. I find that remembering "forward and up," a hint which my body translates into a change of physical relationship between my head and spine, releases tension and makes me better equipped to deal with outside pressures during the day.

The Alexander Technique teacher uses a very light touch, applying gentle pressure with his hands at the base of the head which changes the balance of the head on the neck. The neck muscles are allowed to lengthen which permits the head to come forward and up out of the shoulders. There are also exercises which one can practice alone which aid in producing the effects of the Alexander Technique. I recommend Judith Stransky and Robert B. Stone's book, *The Alexander Technique—Joy in the Life of Your Body* for anyone who is interested in discovering some of the benefits which Alexander originally felt himself after hours of experimenting with his mirrors. After a while of consciously suggesting to yourself, "Let the neck be free, to let the head go forward and up, and let the back lengthen and widen," it will become an unconscious pattern of movement which will affect all of your movements.

We can see this relationship in nature if we observe the movement of animals and babies. But, for various reasons, as we grow older, we habitually pinch the back of the neck and the lower back, which has profound effects both physically and psychologically. This automatic constricting of muscles is called the "startle response." It is caused by gravity, aging, a lack of exercise, and sometimes disease. Although stress is the cause of constricting those muscles, we can make an active choice to "inhibit" that habitual muscular response. "Inhibition" is a word which is key in the study of Alexander Technique. It means a conscious choice over a habitual response. So as Alexander prepared to begin to recite, he inhibited the pattern of the head "down and back" and chose instead "forward and up."

As highly evolved organisms, we live in a world filled with situations which impact upon us in a way which can produce tension or stress, but because our intellect is highly evolved, we are capable of choosing to respond to these stimuli in a different way. The Alexander Technique teaches us that we are capable of stopping and choosing a different physical response to a situation. Because the body is such a sensitive network of nerves and muscles, particularly in the area of the head and neck, this can mean a great change in the way your whole body feels.

It is important to take advantage of learning from a trained teacher of the Alexander Technique. This is not a simple position, like the stiff and unnatural result one observes when a strict teacher orders a child to "Stand up straight!"

The shoulders can reveal a lot about a person, unless he's wearing shoulder pads, and even then the padding sometimes just accentuates the message. When the shoulders are pulled forward, as if sheltering the heart, we see a person who is withdrawn, afraid of being touched emotionally and, in general, someone who doesn't have a very good self-concept. Sometimes girls learn to round their shoulders when they are adolescents because they are self-conscious about their newly developing breasts. Raised shoulders are a clue that the person is carrying a lot of excess tension, or that he is trying to put on a facade to intimidate others. Shoulders which are thrown back, thrusting the chest forward, convey the message of pride or vitality, or openheartedness. Sometimes this same position conveys a feeling of boastfulness or defiance.

When the shoulders are pulled forward, as if sheltering the heart, we see a person who is withdrawn, afraid of being touched emotionally.

My right shoulder curls in—a result of my scoliosis—and

when it was pointed out to me, I had to consciously pull that shoulder down and back. It felt as if I were thrusting the right side of my chest forward to correct the curl in. There was a feeling of confidence suggested by the new position. The old, curled in position felt comfortable and normal, but it also felt safe and hidden, whereas the adjusted position felt as if I were putting myself forward—making a statement that was positive and confident. There was also a mental association which was very vivid which surfaced as I became used to this new way of holding my body. I recognized a defensiveness in my response to a friend who shared with me her successes, personal discoveries, and triumphs. I would never have admitted to it, but there was a sense that I needed to respond competitively to her, rather than sharing her eagerness and joy. When I opened my chest by letting my shoulder come back and down, there was a feeling of acceptance, both of myself and therefore by implication, of my friend. It was almost as if, by exposing my full torso, I was able to express myself more completely and receive the expressions of others more openly.

Interpreting body language involves looking at the entire person to see what the whole body is communicating. It's not enough to look at someone whose shoulders are back with the chest thrust forward and deduce that this person is a braggart. This same person might collapse in at the solar plexus which would suggest something about how he feels about his personal power. Every part of the body is connected and makes sense as a whole whose parts are supporting, compensating, and impacting on the expression of every other part. We need to guard against being overly simplistic and offering facile explanations to what we think we are observing about some aspect of body language. But the study of body language offers a wealth of information about how we feel about ourselves and the world in which we live.

We encounter the world with our hands and use them to make contact with other people; consequently they reveal a great deal about ourselves. The hands are indicators of whether we are relaxed or tense, whether we have devoted our lives to hard, manual labor in the sun, or whether we have been sheltered from

PHOTO COURTESY OF JUST COMMUNICATIONS

What we all strive for is the ability to gesture as easily and naturally as we do in our normal, everyday lives.

the elements and use them for more delicate, intricate work. They tremble when we are nervous or afraid. They are relaxed and open and rest with the palms up and vulnerable when we feel safe and calm. If we are angry or tense, we clench them tightly shut. When we feel an overabundance of energy and enthusiasm, our hands fly to contribute expression to our verbal communication. Even when we talk on the phone, we find that our hands contribute gestures to someone who does not see them. They are an extension of ourselves, and they have the ability to communicate eloquently. They fidget with objects or clothing when we feel inadequate to the situation, and they may touch our face and hair in an effort to reassure ourselves that we are all right.

Many people worry about their hand gestures when they are in front of a group of people. We have all seen speakers who, we suspect, have written into their notes to hold up a finger in the air to emphasize a particular point. This type of gesture is unnatural, arbitrary, and only underscores the self-consciousness of the speaker. On the other hand, when we observe politicians, we come to recognize them almost as much for their gestures as for their voices. Dana Carvey of the television show *Saturday Night Live* created a wonderful characterization of George Bush with elaborate and meaningless hand gestures which imitate this former President's particular style. What we all strive for is the ability to gesture as easily and naturally as we do in our normal, everyday lives. Unfortunately, standing in front of a group of people and speaking to them is not a normal situation, and our hands, precisely because they are such personal and expressive statements of who we are, often seem to become paralyzed or to have a life of their own. It may seem to take an act of enormous will and strength just to lift one's hands from the podium to make a gesture. You may find that once you have lifted your hand up to make an emphatic gesture, you repeat that same gesture over and over again for no reason.

A good thing to do as a public speaker is to shake your hands before you go on to release any feeling of tension. Then forget about them. If you are relaxed and confident, your hands will express that. If not, rest them on the podium or hold them easily at about waist level. It is a natural response in a situation where you feel in danger to cover the genital area with your hands. Athletes often stand this way when they are at attention on the court before a game. This is a reflex which is basic, because we are creatures who instinctively protect ourselves from attack. Recognize that, although you may feel uncomfortable and exposed in a public speaking situation, you are probably not in danger. By releasing your hands from this protective stance, we allow ourselves to draw more freely on the powerful energy which has its source in our reproductive organs. When our hands are unlocked, we are free to go beyond self-preservation toward self-expression. If your hands are at your sides or easily held about waist level, they are available to you if you want to gesture. The energy in your body is flowing easily and freely, without any locks, and your hands, as extensions of the rest of your body, are able to work with you.

Weak, ineffectual gestures, or over-choreographed, stilted gestures are worse than communication which is simple, direct, and unadorned. Some of the most powerful performances on the stage occur when the actor is absolutely still. We find ourselves riveted to the face, the words, and the intent of the speaker. The use of hand gestures is not going to make a weak, ineffectual person appear stronger or more convincing. If a person is confident, if the voice is strong, and the intention is clear, absolute stillness will appear to add to that person's self-composure and power. So don't worry about your hands. As you become more confident, your hands will become more truthfully and naturally expressive.

Eighty percent of communication is non-verbal, and I've learned that the communication which I listen to the most, which gives the most accurate information to me, is that which is non-verbal. I was sitting on a very low stool in the rehearsal hall at the end of the second day's work on a play when the attractive leading man came up to me, stood directly in front of me, about eighteen inches away, looking down at me with direct eye-contact. It wasn't difficult for me to understand his overtly sexual message which I immediately neutralized by standing up and meeting his gaze at an even level.

Eighty percent of communication is non-verbal.

Your body derives energy from various sources. When you are communicating in front of a large group of people, you use a lot of energy from the diaphragm to support the breath and voice. You also feel that your throat is warm and vibrating with the act of verbal expression. Sometimes when involved in an intellectual activity, during a lecture for instance, the brain is the most energized area of the body. When you are deeply touched by an emotional scene, when you are feeling tender and loving, it feels almost as if your heart is leaping out of your body. These energy centers are described and specifically located in the Indian system of chakras. A general overview of this system will help you to understand how the body fuels itself and what source of energy you draw on at a particular moment. You can recognize how someone is more directed by a particular type of energy than someone else. And you can graphically see how that impacts on the way a person holds his body and moves through space. Thus you can learn a great deal about the kind of people you encounter every day. When there is a great deal of tension held at one energy center, or chakra, you can use your understanding of the chakras to help you understand what this person is protecting, or what kind of pain he may have experienced to cause him to adopt an habitual pattern of holding his body.

Very specific energies are localized in particular parts of the human anatomy. The Indian system of chakras divides the areas into seven main centers. Starting at the first chakra, we have the root chakra, located at the perineum. We recognize descriptive terms like "anal-retentive" or "tight-ass". Those whose life energy is blocked at the first chakra are primarily concerned with survival. When the human animal is preoccupied with survival, everything else recedes into the background. It's impossible for many people in poor, Third World countries to think beyond where the next meal is coming from. In a war situation, where life hangs precariously from moment to moment, thoughts of aesthetics and fashion are frivolous and unimportant. The need for safety and security, the will to survive is the most basic of human forces.

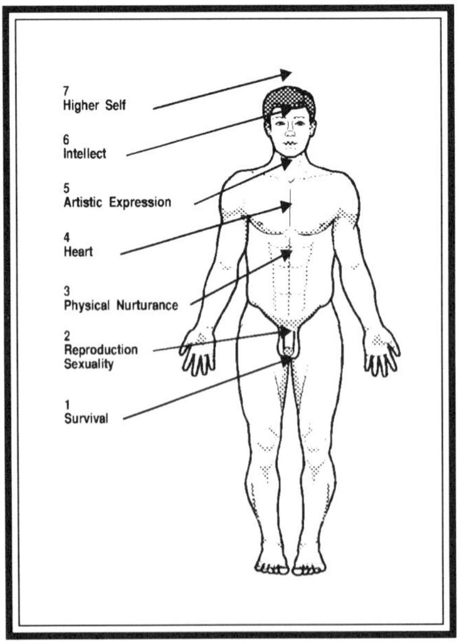

The second chakra is located at the reproductive organs, and understandably, the focus is on sex and self-perpetuation. When we look at other creatures, we see, in a less complicated way, how strong this desire to reproduce is. In fact, with other animals, the sexual act is for the purpose of reproduction. When the female is fertile, the pair mates. When there is high infant mortality, there are more babies in the litter to increase the chance of the species surviving. And among the human population, birth control is not a method which is practiced when children are needed to help search for or cultivate food.

Apart from reproduction, the second chakra is the source of the powerful force of libido. Sexual energy has the ability to fuel an enormous drive when one is attracted to another. The provocative and stylized posing of Mae West emphasized her sexual energy. The gyrations and energetic, pulsing choreography of many rock bands are designed to drive the nubile, young targeted audience into a frenzy of desire and heat. In the movie, *All Of Me,* Lily Tomlin's character was inhabiting the body of a lawyer, played by Steve Martin. When she was forced to act through his body in the courtroom, she expressed what she thought was typical macho-male body language, centered at this second chakra, by drawing attention to his genitals.

The solar plexus is the seat of the third chakra and is associated with the ego and concerns about physical strength or nurturance. One explanation for obesity is that there is an unconscious need to take up space, to command a larger area to accommodate oneself. Conversely, there are overweight people who, out of a sense of unworthiness, compensate by feeding the body too much food. If there are feelings of insecurity or lack, either materially or emotionally, there may be a desire to substitute a need to fill up with food instead. Because this is the seat of great physical strength and energy, it is also the source of fuel when we speak or sing. The breath is supported by the diaphragm.

In a sense, all of the first three chakras are concerned with survival on a physical level. When we are secure, safe, confident, and nourished, our interest can proceed to more emotional and spiritual levels.

The fourth chakra is the heart center and is the metaphorical seat of altruistic love. People who are generous and magnanimous express themselves in an open-hearted way, often physically leading with their heart. Check out Leo Buscaglia. His famous hugs are literally the pressing of his heart to yours. When Luciano Pavarotti has finished an aria in concert, and the audience bravos his magnificent voice, he spreads his arms wide, as if he is opening up his heart completely to receive the adulation of his audience and to give them, just as completely, his love. When experiencing grief and sorrow, it feels as if our hearts are huge, and there is an unconscious desire to press one's hands to the chest, as if to help contain the enormous emotion. When some people experience extreme disappointments or tragedy in life, and their spirit is weak or broken by the strain, the chest often sinks in, so that the torso is concave. The person forms a protective shell where the heart is buried deeper inside the body.

Artistic expression is connected to the fifth chakra, which is located at the throat. Sometimes we feel great emotion and get choked up, unable to express in words the depth of passion we feel. In Martha Graham's dance and in her work with actors on movement, she encouraged the opening of the throat area, which is a display of trust and vulnerability in the animal kingdom.

The sixth chakra is referred to as the third-eye point between the brows and is the spiritual center—our connection with the divine. The intellect is also associated with this part of the anatomy. We all know people who are so intellectual that their head seems to be dissociated from the rest of their body. When I'm worried or very concentrated, I have frown lines between my eyes—an unpleasant reminder that my energy is blocked at this chakra.

Finally, the seventh chakra is actually above the head and represents our Higher Self and our participation with the Divine. In the paintings of the saints, the artist often depicts a halo of light surrounding the head of the figure to signify the holiness of the person. There are people who are able to see an aura emanating from very spiritual people. In moments of spiritual ecstacy, the body seems to be left behind as the spirit soars.

The study of chakras offers us a way of understanding people and what makes them tick. When I saw a young woman walking down the street, leading with her head well in front of the rest of her body, I inferred that she probably had a very technical job which required a great deal of mental concentration. It wouldn't surprise me if she lacked easy access to her emotions. She lacked physical grace, which is one of the benefits derived from physically challenging pastimes. I would guess that she was not an athletic person. Therefore, I would communicate with her intellectually rather than emotionally. And I certainly wouldn't expect her to suggest a meeting after a swim at the YWCA. Going back to the situation in the rehearsal hall, if I responded using second chakra energy to the actor who was coming on to me, that is, if I had leaned back to open up my lower abdomen and gently rolled around a bit to get comfortable, I could expect him to escalate the sexual flirtation even more.

As an actress, I'm always observing people, keeping a mental file for possible use in developing a character later on. When I see someone who has a particular pattern of holding his body, and I want to investigate what that posture suggests about the person, I assume that posture in a conscious attempt to get more information about him by seeing what the posture suggests to me. Why is it that we habitually encounter our world in a particular way, with shoulders hunched, pelvis thrust forward, neck tucked in, etc.?

I notice that the person who lives above me walks with a very heavy step. When I assume that walk myself, I feel purposeful and determined. I recognize the term "grounded," and the person who walks like this is, in a sense, more connected to physical reality than someone who walks lightly on her toes, barely touching the earth.

How perceptive are you of the physical way that people manifest themselves?

I observed a young lawyer at a workshop whose upper torso was immobile with his shoulders held high. There was no sign of breathing because it was so shallow, and even when his back and shoulders were massaged, he continued to hold himself rigid. This posture feels almost like a fortress wall erected to protect oneself. When I hold myself like this and breathe shallowly, I feel timid, cautious, and wary.

When you communicate with others, you communicate with all of them, not just with their words. You touch them at all levels, and you offer all of yourself in your communication, whether you like it or not. How perceptive are you of the physical way that people manifest themselves? You can become more sensitive to what they communicate about themselves before they say a word, and you can influence the quality of your communication with them in the way you em-body who you are. I would approach the person upstairs in a different way than the lawyer at the workshop. Taking into consideration the body language of each, I would adjust myself to them. I would be more likely to be earthy, practical, and direct with my upstairs neighbor, whereas I would approach the lawyer gently, carefully allowing him to take the lead in conversation before I tried to influence him.

As an exercise to sensitize my students to their own body language and their ability to read the body language of others, I have them assume the character of someone else. I have some "character cards" on which I've described various people. One by one my students stand in front of the class and then walk across the room as the character suggested on the card. Then the class shares what they observe of this character. It is remarkable how much information we can pick up from someone before they say a word. You can try some of these on for size. Have fun creating these characters, and don't be afraid to be bold!

- Physical fitness instructor—29 years old—an evangelist for fitness—her body is her temple—very conscious of environment and how she is affected by "vibes"—very positive outlook no matter what the situation.

- Housewife—35 years old—upper middle class—no children but wants children—married to Wall St. broker—would like outside job—intelligent—depressed—self-absorbed.

• Salesman—22 years old—lower middle class—personable—needs money to pay off debts—fiancé won't marry him until he's solvent—charmer—always has been good athlete—fairly bright.

• Executive—32 years old—upper class—very motivated—unmarried—very physically fit—on his way to being president of company—won't settle for less—every moment of his day is scheduled.

• Secretary—28 years old—unattractive and overweight—unmarried—wishes she were married—very hard worker—gets embarrassed when talking to anyone—does needlework and watches television in spare time.

• Communications specialist—45 years old—charismatic—speaks regularly at workshops all over country on effective communication within relationships—inspired—happy spending time alone—never bored.

• Bartender in exclusive disco bar in New York City—25 years old—gorgeous and knows it—makes most of his tips from women who would like to know him better—ambitious to be wealthy and live the life of the rich.

• Scientist—38 years old—has been working alone in same laboratory on same area of inquiry for five years—being considered for grant and needs grant to be able to complete very important experiments—not conscious of personal appearance or much of the surrounding environment.

• Activist/Revolutionary—18 years old—angry about animal rights issues, Pentagon overspending, nuclear waste, etc.—devotes life to informing others, protesting, trying to change world—not concerned about material wealth, appearances, etc.

• Ballet dancer—has studied since she was six—now she dances professionally with N.Y. City Ballet—she is in the corps, but she has a good chance of being principle dancer in a few years—that is all that is important in her life.

• Street kid—17 years old—stays out of school about as often as he attends—lower class—not motivated towards career—more interested in copping drugs—makes money by selling drugs and sometimes stolen merchandise.

• Officer—works inner city—not a rookie—has seen a lot of life—commands respect on street—a cop because he feels it's important and is committed to being a good cop—nobody fools around with this guy.

• Mother of 18 month old twins—loves children and husband, but sometimes overwhelmed by enormous responsibilities—middle class—intends to go back to teaching someday when kids are older—no time for anything she wants to do.

• Waitress—23 years old—pretty and energetic—loves her job—loves talking to people and giving them good service—simple life philosophy: do good work and smile a lot—uncomplicated life—she's not had many sad days in her life—optimistic.

• Miss America contestant—22 years old—has been competing in beauty pageants since she was 12—sees herself as real good-will ambassador—very competitive—wants to be a fashion consultant, marry, and have two kids.

• Farmer—45 years old—inherited farm from parents who got it from grandparents—mortgaged to the hilt to be able to buy equipment—the land is the most important thing he can give kids—must hang on to it—works around the clock—doesn't complain—gives him fulfillment—married 25 years—4 children.

PHOTO COURTESY OF BEYNCH PRESS

We can choose to be more efficient transmitters and receivers of communication by letting our body be open rather than locked up.

Like a satellite dish which is turned toward the signal it is designed to pick up, we can choose to be more efficient transmitters and receivers of communication by letting our body be open rather than locked up. Receptivity and openness is shown by standing with your arms at your sides, facing the person you're talking to, or when sitting, by letting your body be turned in the direction of the person to whom you're speaking. You might turn your hands palms up, and sit with your torso slightly inclined, with your feet in front of you, flat on the floor.

If you wanted to convey a more authoritarian posture, stand up, even if the others in the room are seated. I once was at a television station to do a promotional piece for a theater company. There were a number of other people who were also there as guests on the same magazine-type show. It was very early in the morning, and those of us from the theater company were a bit disgruntled at having to wait, especially since we had had a performance the night before, and we weren't given the option of doing our bit on tape at another time. When the host of the show came into the green room, he took control of the situation by making himself the focus of everyone's attention. He remained standing and became the moderator of all the separate groups in the room, talking to the group as a whole and acting like the social director of a cruise ship. Just by standing, moving about the room, and taking up space, he was able to control the situation and exert his authority.

If the situation is your office, the same principle of taking up space applies: let there be space between your chair and your desk so that your body can be seen. You may lean back in the chair and still control the desk area by resting one arm on the desk. You show that you inhabit the space; it is yours and you feel confident about belonging there.

If you are in a situation where you want it to be clear that you are not trying to usurp someone's authority, or you do not want to be seen as a leader of the group, physicalize that attitude by sitting on the periphery of the room. If you are at a table, let your hands remain in your lap rather than resting them on the table. Sit erect, with your feet flat on the floor or crossed at the ankles and hidden under your chair. Try sitting this way, and you'll see that it's not easy to feel much energy or power. The position is physically passive and reflects a passive attitude.

On the other hand, someone who is presenting ideas, wishing to influence or persuade, sits in a "ready" position, with the body weight inclining forward, ready to stand up and move. The hands are visible on the desk, aiding in the presentation and persuasion with effective gestures, or resting relaxed and gently open.

In a more general and more truthful way, we eventually find that one's body language is capable of much more expression, subtlety, and elegance than can be described or codified. We all have the ability and the instinctive knowledge to eloquently express ourselves using words, gestures, facial expressions, and body language. Watch a baby and notice how close to the surface each emotion is expressed. The fluidity and clarity of the baby's non-verbal language is something which we are all born with but which we've learned to suppress because of fear. "Big boys don't cry," "Control yourself," "Don't show off," "Nice girls don't flirt," etc., are lessons which eventually take their toll, leaving us with the illusion of safety in bodies which are unexpressive and lifeless.

Your natural liveliness, expressiveness, and freedom of movement can be reclaimed if you want it back. Learn to relax and consciously focus your energy, and remember that those who are willing to appear foolish are the ones who will not look like fools.

The more you willingly and consciously allow yourself to be expressive, the easier it will be for you to experience the freedom which comes from communicating physically, emotionally, mentally and spiritually all the time.

Chapter 3 The Body/Mind Connection

We generally think in terms of a person's professional success when we hear the term "self-made person." The self-made person is one who perhaps was not born into a wealthy family, and who did not inherit the family business after a period of apprenticeship.

My parents were children of uneducated, poor, hard-working people, and in many ways they are self-made people. They vacation in Africa, China, and Japan, live in Hawaii in an A-frame house overlooking the ocean, spend time each year on their houseboat at Barkley Lake in Kentucky, and thoroughly enjoy life. They both put themselves through school, and my mother, at 18, was the youngest graduate of Millikin College in Decatur, Illinois. She became a leading educator of gifted children and has lectured and written extensively on the subject of gifted children. My father, who at one time worked for Nabisco, eventually owned and operated his own tire and appliance store in my hometown of Charleston, Illinois. They are the kind of people we would describe as self-made.

But in a more comprehensive way, we are all self-made people. Cary Grant said that he imagined the person he wanted to become and then became the embodiment of that person. While some of us live our lives as victims of poverty or disease, or carry the shadow of a deprived childhood with us throughout life, forever attributing our lack of success on past history, others surmount incredible adversity and become productive, inspiring role models. The attitude with which we approach life is crucial. We can choose to actively create ourselves and our lives right now, or we can let ourselves passively respond to our backgrounds, our environment, and the routine succession of days in our lives.

We have discovered how our bodies mirror who we are emotionally, spiritually and mentally, and we have seen how we can gain a wealth of information about people by paying attention to their body language. But we do not need to continue expressing ourselves in the same, habitual ways we've grown accustomed to using. Once we recognize the idiosyncratic ways in which we gesture, hold our body, and use our voice, there is nothing to hold us back from deciding to use other ways to express ourselves, ways in which we present ourselves as more receptive, more authoritative, more vigorous, or as possessing any attitude or quality we wish to project.

A teacher of mine says, "If you always do what you've always done, you'll always get what you've always got!" If you discover that your body language conveys the message that you are overly aggressive and you want to change that, you can! What is more, you will probably discover that, as you grow accustomed to communicating through a more receptive, affirmative posture, you will feel less stressed and will find it less important to assert yourself in aggressive, argumentative ways.

> ***"If you always do what you've always done, you'll always get what you've always got."***

I do not suggest that we all become actors, mastering the art of disguise in order to manipulate those around us. I am extending a challenge to get "un-stuck." Why become a victim of communication habits which you've formed in the past? Assess your strengths and weaknesses as a communicator or public speaker and know that you can move out of the patterns you find less effective and go on to develop better skills which will eventually become natural and habitual for you.

The body and the mind are intimately connected: if we change one, there is a corresponding change which occurs in the other. Have you noticed that you often get sick at a time when you are psychologically worn-out or vulnerable? Good health promotes a happy disposition, and conversely, a happy, empowered disposition is a great vaccine against disease. People who work out know that they can improve their state of mind and their effectiveness on the job after exercising. Instead of deciding not to work out because they don't feel like it, they choose to work out when they feel depressed or lack energy. Instead of passively accepting a state of mind, they decide upon the state of mind they want and do what they know will produce it.

The Method school of acting uses exercises in sense memory, emotional memory, and substitution to produce the psychological and emotional feelings which are appropriate to the actor's character in a scene. The inner emotional experience becomes so real and truthful that the associated physical manifestation is believable and honest.

There are other actors who have a more external approach to acting. They study human behavior and movement and imitate the way people express themselves physically. Because the body and mind are connected, they thereby trigger the emotional responses associated with the particular posture or movement. Both techniques are equally valid, they just take different routes to get to the same goal. The body / mind connection is a two-way street: influence one, and you influence the other.

Some people spend years in analysis and therapy, healing psychological pain by coming to an understanding of the cause of the pain. Previously repressed experiences are remembered and explored and, often, like a lanced wound, the injury begins to heal. But it is possible to move beyond the psychological barrier by changing the physical or material manifestation itself and thereby cause the psychological barrier to break down.

Rolfing, or Structural Integration, is a method of body work which directly affects the muscle tissue, sometimes causing the client to experience emotional pain which has become manifest in a concrete physical expression of the body. Without knowing why, the client may begin to cry as the Rolfer lengthens and moves the muscle tissue. The physical and psychological changes which begin with the Rolfing session continue to evolve long after the client has finished "being Rolfed." Rolfing is based on the principle that there is an inherent pattern and order in the human body and that, through Structural Integration, one can achieve enhanced balance and alignment with gravity.

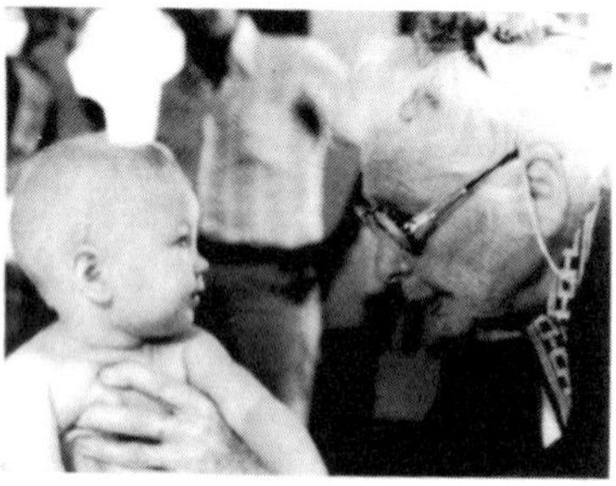

Ida P. Rolf

Ida Rolf was born in New York in 1896, grew up in the Bronx, attended Barnard College, and received her Ph.D. in biological chemistry at Columbia. A friend of hers who had fallen and was, as a result, unable to teach music, recovered after working with Rolf. Rolf began by using hatha yoga as a treatment therapy, stretching and twisting to increase the space at the joints. She was also interested in Alexander Technique and homeopathy. More than curing symptoms, Rolf was interested in helping people to become happier, better functioning individuals. She realized that "structure determines function." Therefore, she knew that it was not enough to mend or straighten broken bones. The muscles surrounding the bones also needed to be treated in order to effect change, otherwise the muscles would simply return to their habitual positions. She saw the interconnectedness of the body—when one area is affected, the rest of the body is affected as well. She believed that "There can be a change of function, a contribution to the health, well-being, wholeness, and functioning of a body through balanced change in structure."

Rolf claimed that the only tool she used was gravity. It is gravity which pulls us down over the years, collapsing our bodies, causing us to lose height as we age. Rolf developed a system which changed the way that the parts of the body join together. The pull of gravity is transmitted through the body in a more economical way, resulting in increased energy. Thus one experiences, after being Rolfed, a sense of lightness and buoyancy. There is a floating feeling which leaves one feeling relaxed, with a heightened sense of awareness.

When you decide to "be Rolfed," you commit yourself to a basic series of from ten to fifteen sessions, each about one hour in length. Most of the time you lie on a padded table while the practitioner works over your body in a systematic way, lengthening, stretching, and applying pressure to the fascia, the tissue which surrounds the muscles.

Many people describe the treatment as painful, and although my practitioner said that I allowed her to use a great deal of pressure, I never experienced pain. I felt like a dry sponge, eager to soak up moisture. The physical sensations were intense and extremely interesting to me. Most of the time it felt good the way it feels good to stretch out your back after bending over.

Many people find that the sessions trigger emotional responses. Because our bodies are repositories for past experiences, becoming the embodied form of our histories, the deep pressure applied during Rolfing releases the memories of events which have been stored in the muscles.

Moshe Feldenkrais, whose techniques incorporating "Awareness Through Movement" and "Functional Integration," promoted improved self-awareness and greater flexibility, as well as increased range of motion, better posture, and better breathing. He said that all negative emotion results in the shortening of the flexor muscles. When these muscles are chronically or habitually flexed, one experiences a feeling of fatigue or depression. So when these chronically flexed muscles are stretched and lengthened, there is a great feeling of release and relief. It isn't necessary to verbally acknowledge or explore the emotional associations you experience during Rolfing with your practitioner, but each Rolfer must have a background in psychology. It is important to give feedback about the physical sensations you experience in order to provide the practitioner with more information about your body. Each session is built on the session before and leads up to what will happen next. Occasionally you will stand up, walk around the room, sit down, etc. in order for the practitioner to observe the adjustments which your body is making. Through the process of Rolfing, you become more aware of how you stand, sit, and walk. One extremely interesting session began for me when my Rolfer, Laurie Latner, looked at photos taken of me as a baby and small child. These pictures clearly showed the same pattern of an out-turned right leg which she could still observe in my present posture.

Structural Integration is more or less "successful" depending on the elasticity of the body and the emotional readiness and receptivity of the individual. Rolfers like to describe the sessions as promoting a direction of change which continues beyond the last session. Ida Rolf said, ". . . changes happen through Rolfing, and it begins to be possible for a body to take on what we consider appropriate adult form. Then the person continues on psychologically, and develops. But until then, no." It is also possible to return to your practitioner for booster visits after you have completed the basic series of treatments.

Many different kinds of people are drawn to Rolfing: athletes, dancers, and musicians who may feel limited by their bodies in their professions, people who are interested in growing psychologically and emotionally, and those of us who are curious about ourselves and eager to learn more about how we function.

We don't need to feel that we are saddled with the way in which we currently express ourselves physically. Change can come in many ways, but one of the most direct ways is by deciding on the change we want and doing it! We can stop rationalizing and give ourselves permission to evolve in other directions. If you want to be more forceful and authoritarian, behave and move in a way which is more powerful. Like Cary Grant, visualize who you want to be, see yourself as that person, hear yourself talk, and feel the way that person would feel.

A few years ago, my closest friend, a professional singer, asked me to sing a duet with her in church. Singing onstage in a musical has always been a high for me. But singing in a church or anywhere my identity was undisguised, not as a character in a show, had always terrified me. I had managed to survive through a few solo lines in some anthems that year, and I was actively confronting my fear of singing. I figured that Linda's invitation was the opportunity I needed to progress further through my terror. (More about stagefright in Chapter 7.) At choir practice the week before the performance, we rehearsed the duet in front of the choir. I had decided to put my hands in my pockets while I sang because that felt comfortable to me. When one of the members of the choir told me that I shouldn't put my hands in my pockets during our performance, I realized that the "director" in me could have given the "actor" in me that direction. When I envisioned Mary Stark, the "singer," I could see the way I wanted to walk, stand, and sing as the "singer." By hiding my hands in my "comfortable" pockets I was copping out, indulging the old vision I had of myself as inadequate and fearful.

It takes effort to change. Habits are seductive. You must be firm to stop the buzz inside your head that says the same negative or less than resourceful chatter about yourself and your environment. Pretend that your mind is a cassette recorder and put in a different tape which repeats new, positive messages. Whenever you hear the old tape, switch "cassettes" and listen to the new one.

Begin to see challenging situations in a different context. Instead of seeing the duet as a terrible ordeal to be endured, I saw it as an opportunity to move beyond my fear of singing in public. Choose to see your world in a way which supports the self-image and life you want. You are right on target, doing exactly what you should be doing in the way it should be done right now. And if you feel uneasy about being able to say this, if it lacks validity in your life as it now stands, then make a change. But *you* make a change, don't allow yourself to be a victim of what you have believed to be overpowering circumstances.

Whenever you hear the old tape, switch "cassettes" and listen to the new one.

When circumstances moved me from New York City to Rochester, New York, as a professional actress, I was less than enthusiastic. I felt that my career was ruined and that there would be no opportunities for me in upper New York state. But I went to work, scheduling interviews, circulating my picture and resume, promoting and re-writing my one-woman-show on Harriet Beecher Stowe, and exploring teaching and directing opportunities for the first time. My career in Manhattan had been limited to extra work in films, showcases, and making the rounds of agents and casting directors, along with all the other out-of-work actors in the city. After a year and a half in Rochester, doing only acting, directing, and teaching jobs, I was making the equivalent of what I was making, working full-time in Manhattan at a retail store. It wasn't long before my career was actually as an actress rather than someone trying to get acting work. I was able to significantly expand my acting, directing, and teaching resumes during the six and a half years I was in upstate New York so that when the time came for me to move to the West Coast, I was armed with extensive experience and impressive commercial credits. Opportunities sometimes come disguised, so we should cultivate the ability to see the hidden potential in the circumstances of our lives.

There is no reason why we can't see our body, our body language, and our communication methods with the same eye for opportunity. If you have areas which are weak, these are the places where you can gain strength. Suppose you have noticed that you don't hold people's attention when you are called upon to make presentations. If you dislike presenting and feel you will bore people, consider the probability that your less-than-eager attitude toward presenting is infectious. If you don't want to be standing there, why should anyone else be enthusiastic about listening to you? Chances are that the way you move up to the podium lacks energy and vitality, and that you are not speaking from the diaphragm, so that your voice is not grounded with energy from the solar plexus. You may lack the nerve to make eye contact with your audience, and consequently, they have little reason to look at you.

Your discouraged, fearful attitude blocks the flow of energy which could enliven your body, mind, and message. By focusing on your breath and letting it be relaxed, by breathing diaphragmatically through the nose, and by consciously relaxing your body from the top of your head to the soles of your feet, you can open your body so that it can freely act as a channel for the energy

PHOTO COURTESY OF JUST COMMUNICATIONS

By focusing on your breath and letting it be relaxed, by breathing diaphragmatically through the nose, and by consciously relaxing your body from the top of your head to the soles of your feet, you can open your body so that it can freely act as a channel.

you need to fuel your presentation. You are, metaphorically, shifting out of reverse into neutral, and as you stand, move to the podium, make eye contact with the audience and begin your presentation, you move forward.

You are also able to add the audience's energy to your own. Actors are very aware of the energy of the audience and the effect it has on the performance. The audience is a creative part of the performance, influencing, in subtle ways, the work of the actor. Even though the actor may not be able to see beyond the lights, he can sense the involvement of the audience. There must be the willingness to be moved by the audience as well as to move the audience. Although the audience is not speaking directly to the presenter or actor, the communication goes in two directions with both sides transmitting and receiving. Tension and fear, which are both manifestations of ego-involvement, limit the easy flow of information so that communication is impaired. The audience senses that they are not part of the performance or the presentation and, like a television set, they mentally turn you off.

You are a presenter or communicator because you have something to say which your audience needs to hear. Your intention as you make your presentation is to fill their need. With that attitude in mind, every moment is purposeful. Your eye contact is a means by which you not only express your information but also pick up cues from the audience. Did they understand that point? Did that particular illustration strike a familiar note for that particular person? Does this idea need elaboration? Fundamentally, you are talking to individuals who are unique and are there to get their needs filled by what you, with your specific expertise and point of view, can give them. If the information alone were important, they could read a book or buy the video!

The more we use our body, the more comfortable and skilled we become in the use of it. If we live sedentary lives, and express ourselves at a desk, behind a computer, and talking into a telephone all day long, is it any wonder that the body gets out of practice in being expressive? A physical exercise program which involves stretching, strengthening, and aerobic movement is essential in order to maintain an efficient, healthy, dynamic, and vitally expressive body. The increased energy you will experience as a result of the exercise program will provide you with more fuel and life-energy and will have a profound and direct

A physical exercise program which involves stretching, strengthening, and aerobic movement is essential in order to maintain an efficient, healthy, dynamic, and vitally expressive body.

PHOTO COURTESY OF JUST COMMUNICATIONS

impact on your public-speaking. Exercise provides an outlet for excess tension and is a stress reducer. As you exercise, you will become more conscious of your body. You will notice tension as it begins to physically manifest itself. You will become more adept in returning to neutral as you learn to coordinate movement and breath. You will also notice more elegance and grace in the way your body expresses itself. As a child learns to play the piano, at first clumsily searching for the right notes on the keyboard, so we start out training our muscles to execute movements. Practice makes perfect. The body and the mind are intimately connected. By becoming more physically fit and learning to breathe diaphragmatically, we become less vulnerable to depression, inertia, and fatigue.

Acting confident and self-assured won't necessarily fool the audience or ourselves when we are called upon to perform or present. But it is within our power to make great changes in the way we think, move, and give verbal and non-verbal expression to our thoughts. Our bodies and our minds are dynamic, constantly changing expressions of who we are, and we can consciously influence the shape of that change.

We grow intellectually by reading, traveling, and participating with the world around us. We grow spiritually through prayer, meditation, contemplation, and communing with nature. We grow physically through exercise, good nutrition, and taking care of our body. And we grow in our ability to communicate with other people by understanding that our intent is to serve them by satisfying the needs of our audience. We have something that they want, and we offer it to them. When our body is healthy and free of tension, and when our intention is to express ourself as fully as possible in order to serve our audience, our body and mind become connected in purpose and can communicate as a unit. The body and its language of physical expression become the substance and the embodiment of the mind's subconscious and conscious thought.

Chapter 4 The Actor's Tools

The cornerstone on which all other acting technique is based is the concept of intention or objective. Acting is not an attitude or an emotion, it is doing, acting, creating. It is a verb rather than a noun or adjective or adverb. The most important question to ask oneself is "What do I want?" This question must be answered with a verb which is active rather than passive. For instance, "I want to seduce" instead of "I want to be pretty." The first statement suggests action and movement, whereas the second suggests a state of being and is therefore static.

Imagine a scene where an unfaithful wife is romantically preoccupied with her lover in her home, under the impression that her husband is gone to work for the day. The husband's car is heard in the driveway, and the lover quickly hides himself in the closet. In the ensuing scene between the husband and wife, the wife wants "to distract her husband from the bedroom," and the husband, acting on a whim, has come home with the intention of "sweeping his wife off her feet." So all of their actions in this scene would be related to their objectives, which are in conflict with each other. Only an amateur actress would settle for playing nervousness in this scene. The actress with an objective would be directed in every moment by her objective. Finally the two characters may both succeed in achieving their objectives by creating a romantic mood for themselves in the livingroom for a change. And all the while the lover is in the closet, or escaping through the bedroom window!

The difference in what the audience sees is, for example, the difference between the form or idea of a cake and the actual baking of a cake. If we settle for an approximation of the form itself, we may end up with a picture of a cake, the word "cake," my idea of cake rather than your idea of cake, bad cake, stale cake, birthday cake, wedding cake, a cake of soap, etc. Whereas, if we have the intention to bake a cake, we start at the beginning, with the proper ingredients, mixing them together, pouring them into the pan, and placing the pan in the oven. If we do the actions correctly, we will come up with a cake.

In the preceding example of the husband and wife, instead of the wife doing the standard, cliché gestures of wringing her hands and fiddling with her buttons, we see the actions which tell us that she is doing everything she can to distract her husband. Her nervousness will be apparent through her actions and the result will be that we see a person believably dealing with a situation rather than an actress posing.

If my concern is to be pretty, who is to say that what I consider pretty is what you consider pretty? If I try "to be pretty," what can I do? Smile, purse my lips together, pat my hair, bat my eyelashes? Do those behaviors have anything to do with "pretty"? If, however, my intention is "to seduce," I will catch the eye of the other person, I will invite him, directly or indirectly, to follow me, and I will exhaust every possibility of enticement until my objective is satisfied.

A simple exercise which clarifies the importance of an objective is "Knocking." I give each student a card which describes a situation. Then each student goes to the door of the room and knocks as the person suggested on their card. Here are some examples for you to try. Notice how in each situation the objective is a different one, and dramatically affects the simple action of knocking.

• You're looking for your dog which has been missing for two days. You're asking all the people in the apartment complex where you live if they've seen him.

• You're the police and you're busting this apartment for drugs.

• You just found out that you won the lottery, and you're going to tell your nearest neighbor the good news.

• You have discovered an extensive cheating ring at your school and are at the principle's office to report it.

• The neighbors are having a party, and it's 3:00 a.m., and you have a job interview this morning and can't sleep.

• You're picking up your girlfriend before the prom.

• You are leaving a May basket at the house of your sweetheart.

• You have made plans to go out with a friend in the middle of the night, and you're picking up the friend now. You must not wake the friend's parents.

• While you were out walking, you saw a neighborhood grocery store being held up. You ran to the nearest house, and you want to use the phone to call the police.

• You are picking up a friend for an early morning jog, but you'd really rather be in bed.

• You are a parent trying to get into the room where your daughter has been with her boyfriend. The lights are out, and you can't hear them talking.

• You're about to see your best friend for the first time in three years, and over the years you've lost touch with each other.

• There is a fire two floors down and you're trying to wake up the people on your floor.

• It's cold and wet, and your car stalled two miles down the road. This is the first farmhouse you've come to.

• You're selling Mary Kay cosmetics door to door.

• You accidently broke the neighbor's picture window while playing baseball, and you've come to apologize.

When choosing your objective, you must make it something which is important to you. This will mean that the way you "play" your objective will be filled with energy, vitality, and intensity. For instance, if you are just selling cosmetics as a way of making extra money, you probably won't make as many sales as you would if you were trained to believe that the company you represent is ranked third in your life, only behind your family and your religion. If you are on your way to earning a pink Cadillac, you knock with more enthusiasm and eagerness than a half-hearted, disillusioned salesman. You can work on increasing the intensity behind your objective with the "Who Sent This Package" exercise which a teacher, Tom McNally, taught me.

Each student, while holding a package or something to represent a package, creates a subtext or context which leads up to the question, "Who sent this package?" For instance, I work at the embassy and have received a parcel, which is ticking, wrapped in brown paper. I will repeat the same line over and over again, escalating the intention with each repetition and finally end the exercise by saying, "Who sent this package." So I might choose to say, "It's ticking!" over and over. My objective is to figure out how to open the package without detonating the bomb. I would become increasingly agitated with each repetition of "It's ticking!" while remembering my objective, until I finally end the exercise by asking, "Who sent this package?"

Another exercise which I use with my students to help them understand the idea of intention or objective is "Happy Birthday." I give the instructions that they are to sing "Happy Birthday" three times, once to a baby, once to a lover, and once to their dying mother. Try it. Decide first what your objective is in each situation. Are you in a hospital bed on the day you gave birth to this baby you are holding? Your intention might be "to pledge your undying love to your daughter." Are you calling up your lover with whom you quarrelled two months ago in a gesture of apology? Your intention might be "to smooth things over." Are you at the bedside of your unconscious and dying mother, knowing that she may still be able to hear you? Your intention might be "to connect with her one last time."

This exercise often marked the most significant point in the series of classes I taught. When the students committed themselves to their objective, their imaginations were freed, and there was a loss of self-consciousness. They were concentrated on their objective rather than themselves, and the results were quite moving to both the student and to the observers. These were not actors, by the way, but professional people who were interested in learning to become more effective communicators. It takes courage to get up in front of a group of people. But armed with a good, strong objective, you have a tool to help you. You keep your objective in mind as the focus of your concentration and keep coming back to it whenever you feel distracted by the public speaking situation.

We have agreed that our primary purpose as communicators is to serve the audience or the listener by giving them what they need. This is the general objective, which you achieve by deciding on a subject which is of interest to the audience and which you can illuminate for them. You must believe that you know something about the subject which would benefit your audience to know. Therefore, it is your responsibility to learn as much about your subject as possible. The more you know, the more confidence you will have in speaking. You will generate more interest in your audience, and your audience will feel more relaxed and trust you to inform and educate them.

You must believe that you know something about the subject which would benefit your audience to know.

Prepare yourself by going to your library and reading all that is offered, not only in the card catalog but also in the Reader's Guide to Periodical Literature, in order to have as current an understanding about your subject as possible. The research librarian is a great resource. It is this person's job to assist you. I have found that I am always welcomed whenever I present the librarian with my subject for investigation. They seem to relish the challenge of a new area of research and will readily lead you to books and periodicals which will focus on the topic which you are investigating. Learn

---

Learn what the opposing point of view is so that you are armed in advance for questions from skeptics.

---

what the opposing point of view is so that you are armed in advance for questions from skeptics. Keep a record handy of your sources of information to give to those who are interested in following up on your talk or presentation.

Decide what are the most important points to make. If there is a central argument which you are presenting, what do you need to establish first in order to present that argument? Keep in mind that any listening audience can absorb only so much at one sitting. Keep it simple. If you have a lot of figures to present, use a visual aid to reinforce the numbers. Visual aids can be very effective in any presentation if they are clear and are used in an adept way. Make sure that you are comfortable using the visuals and that the room you are using is equipped with the space, lighting, and electrical requirements necessary to make your visuals effective.

When you are constructing your presentation, ask yourself frequently what your objective is while you are researching, writing and rehearsing your talk. If you are not fulfilling that objective at every point of your presentation, you will need to refine your material and get back to the point of your thesis. Keep in mind that your job is to "dovetail" your presentation to fit the needs of your audience. The more perfectly you can make the objective fulfill the needs of the audience, the happier and more satisfied they will be, and the more successful you will be in your communication.

Be bold. If your presentation seems boring to you, perhaps the objective isn't important enough. Up the ante. Instead of making a presentation to "show" how your advertising agency is better than the one the client is currently employing, decide that your objective is to "explode" the current marketing expectations of the company and to "challenge" the prospective client with exponential growth possibilities. Your presentation will be much more interesting and persuasive if what you are trying to do is to "explode" and "challenge" instead of just "show."

Motivation is the fuel which the actor knows is necessary in order to make the objective work. If you have no interest in persuading your audience, you won't be as effective as the speaker who stands to gain a 10% commission from each sale. It isn't necessary for the gain to be financial in order for it to be effective. If you believe in your product, you have faith that your audience will be better served by it than by your competitor's product. If your talk is a travelogue, you believe that the listeners will be enriched by the information. And if your purpose is to entertain, you may feel, like Norman Cousins, that laughter is the great healer.

One of my acting teachers told the story of Sonya, a student of the great Russian acting teacher, Stanislavski, who was given the exercise of looking for an imaginary piece of jewelry on a parlor set. Sonya, imagining herself to be a brilliant actress, proceeded to show the other students how one acts "searching" by indicating her objective with exaggerated grimaces and gestures, being careful to keep her face to the audience, stepping prettily, and positioning herself gracefully against the furniture pieces. Stanislavski then asked her to loan him her antique ring, told her to close her eyes, and hid the ring in his pocket. He then instructed her to repeat the exercise. The search which ensued made it clear that Sonya wanted her ring back and that she intended to comb the entire set, stepping very carefully for fear that she might inadvertently step on the ring and break it. This was a motivated objective which made the difference in her audience's belief in her objective.

Decide why it is that you are delivering your presentation. It isn't good enough to say that it is your turn to deliver the keynote speech for your organization. Your audience will detect your ambivalence. Why should they care about your topic if you don't? Perhaps you are clear that you need to overcome your fear of speaking before groups and you know that if you make this presentation, you will forever obliterate that fear. The better your motivation, the more personal the stakes are, the more fuel your objective will have.

Your motivation must be more than an intellectualized idea in order for it to serve you. You must be fueled by your motivation every moment you speak. Every point of your presentation must be made because of a present need in your audience which you must address in order to satisfy them. If your presentation is a speech which is written and rehearsed until its form is committed to memory, you must not fall into the trap of rattling off what you already know and are convinced of. You must present the material as if each point is being presented because it is necessary in order to enlighten and persuade your audience.

Another good exercise given to me by Tom McNally is one called Monologue/Dialogue. Take your prepared speech and work out questions or comments theoretically presented by members of your hypothetical audience as you are speaking. These questions must require your response which is, in fact, the next statement of your prepared presentation. Keep in mind that what you say must arise out of an immediate need of the audience which you satisfy in your speech.

In a *New Yorker* profile of the comedian, Jackie Mason, he talks about this relationship between himself and his audience. "There are differences in every audience. Some comedians are boring because they aren't in touch with the audience's mind. Onstage, it's as if you were carrying on a conversation with the audience, even though you are doing all the talking. You have to adjust to the reactions of the audience. It's an evolved awareness. Timing is a knowledge and awareness of the mood of an audience. There are performers who bully an audience. I try to involve the audience emotionally in my message. They have to believe what you're saying. You set up a basic premise, and if they are convinced of its truth, it becomes a living experience to them, and they are ready to be moved by laughter. Part of being fascinating to an audience is being unpredictable. You have to make them anxious to hear what you say next."

Try the Monologue/Dialogue exercise with this monologue from Studs Terkel's *Working*. First read it aloud.

Herb: I'm the president and chief executive of this corporation. I have a lavish office, two secretaries, a private dining room with a private chef. I couldn't be more secure, right? I don't know of any situation in the corporate world where an executive is sure of his job from moment to moment. Oh, we put on a front: "Nothing can happen to me, I'm too important." But the fear is there. You can smell it. So, I sit in my lavish office and eat Gelusil by the minute.

When a top executive is fired, the shock is tremendous. He doesn't know what hit him. Immediately, his Cadillac is taken away from him; his WATS line is taken away from him. Even his phone at home stops ringing. Everybody shuns him because they don't want to be associated with him. Bingo, he's dead.

We hired a Vice-President. He was with us about six months and he was totally inadequate. I called him into the office and told him he was through, gave him a nice severance pay. He broke down and cried. "What did I do wrong? Please don't do this to me. My daughter's getting married next month. How am I going to face people?" He cried, and he cried, and he cried. But we couldn't keep him on, we had to let him go . . .

Now, define the overall objective. Perhaps Herb wants to "protect his territory." So the first line might be said in answer to the unverbalized question, "Do you have job security?" He answers, somewhat defensively, "I'm the president and chief executive of this corporation." The next unasked question could be, "What perks do you get in a job like yours?" To which Herb answers, "I have a lavish office, two secretaries, a private dining room with a private chef." He could be bragging, or he might be affecting an air of nonchalance. What question could elicit the response of "I couldn't be more secure, right?" How about, "So you don't have anything to worry about, do you?" Continue on with the rest of the monologue.

The advantage of working with your own speech in this way is that every moment will be alive to the audience, as if you are getting the fuel for your speech from them, answering their questions and responding to their non-verbal cues as you go. There is an impulse before every sentence which is your remembrance of the unasked question which acts as the stimulus for everything you say. You are preparing yourself for the real situation when you are in front of a real audience which reacts to what you say. You won't be thrown by their reactions and will be more capable of "folding" in their responses, adding them to the "mix" of your speech.

The New Age writer and mystic, Ram Dass, uses the term "Be Here Now." In using the Monologue/Dialogue exercise, you approach your speech not as a lump of words which you unload on the audience, but like a string of pearls which you finger one by one. Each moment of your speech is a pearl to be considered and appreciated individually both by you and your audience. Like Jackie Mason, let your audience become emotionally involved with what you say, and they will become contributing factors in your public speaking experience.

One common pitfall of bad actors is known as "acting in a vacuum." Instead of responding to the input of the other actors in the scene, letting them color the delivery of the speech, some actors get enamored of their interpretation of their role to the point where they are unaffected by what is happening around them. There is no feeling that what the character is doing is motivated by the actions on stage. We get the feeling that the actor is more interested in presenting the speech and listening to his own voice than living within the reality of the scene.

If you are adept in the technique of the Monologue/Dialogue exercise, your speech will have the effect of a conversation or interaction with your audience which will make them feel involved in your subject. Give yourself the image of being propelled from point to point by the curiosity of your listeners.

The term "concentration" as used by the actor is a noun which stands for the concept known in acting theory as the Point of Concentration. What is the focus of attention? For the child who is trying to divert his mother's attention by singing a song at the top of his lungs, the concentration is the whimpering puppy which he is hiding in his closet. For the wife who is attempting to hurry her husband home from the office, the concentration is the surprise party which is awaiting his arrival. For the speaker, the Point of Concentration is whatever will give focus and stability when you might otherwise diffuse your energy due to nerves, fear, excitement, or distractions from your audience or environment. Your concentration might be the motor home which you will win if you make this sale, or the commendation from your manager if you secure this client, or the votes you need to win the election. It does not serve you well to have your concentration be the sweat on your brow, the pencil you are holding, or the good-looking young person in the second row.

I have discovered and imparted to many astonished and grateful students that an effective Point of Concentration can always be found in the breath. Before I perform, as I prepare myself for a scene or a presentation or an audition, I calm myself

PHOTO COURTESY OF JUST COMMUNICATIONS

An effective Point of Concentration can always be found in the breath.

down and bring my focus to the center of my being by observing the inhalation and exhalation of my breath at the point where it enters and exits my nostrils. It may sound simplistic and silly, but try it. Do not attempt to change your breath by lengthening or shortening the breath. Just observe it. If you should have a momentary lapse of memory, observing your breath will calm you. Remember your objective, fuel that objective with your motivation, and focus your presentation by means of your Point of Concentration. Your audience will know that you have everything under control and will trust you to continue when you are ready. Meanwhile, you will be refreshing yourself and enabling yourself to locate your place and continue with competence and energy.

An additional benefit of breath awareness is that when the breath is flowing easily and diaphragmatically, there is a corresponding freeing up which occurs on a physical and emotional level. You may have observed yourself in an upsetting situation holding your breath in a desperate attempt to restrain yourself from crying. You force yourself to breathe shallowly, and when the tears finally break through, the sobbing is the release of the breath which has been held back. As the tears subside, the breath returns to its normal inhalation and exhalation. Knowing this can aid the actor in tapping into the emotional truth in a scene. "Breathe it in" is a conscious command to acknowledge the emotional climate and to digest it as the character. When your breath is relaxed and even, you are more capable of responding spontaneously, honestly, and fully. Your body and mind are more available to receive the impressions of your audience to what you are saying, and from that informed vantage point, you, as the speaker, will be more able to adjust your style, dynamic range, and available information in order to meet the audience's needs.

The practice of yoga postures is intimately related to the study of breath awareness. The impressive contortions and extreme demonstrations of physical elasticity and grace are only the outward extreme manifestations of this discipline. What the yogi understands is that the degree to which an *asana* or posture is executed is not the purpose of the exercise. It is rather the self-awareness of the student within the posture which is the field of inquiry. The inhalation and exhalation are as much a part of the movement and the stillness as the position itself. Through focusing on the breath, the student quietly observes the effect which the *asana* produces.

It may require some concentrated attention on your breath away from the public speaking situation to make it an automatic Point of Concentration when you are behind the podium or on a stage. So begin by lying down on the floor at home with your right hand on your chest and your left hand on your diaphragm, the hollowed area at the base of your rib cage. Relax and observe if your right hand is moving up and down as you breathe. If you are breathing diaphragmatically, your left hand will be the one moving. As you continue to relax, you can begin a Complete Breath which will involve both the diaphragm and the upper torso. Breathe in through your nose, filling the diaphragm first, and noticing your left hand moving as you do. Then, as you continue to fill your lungs, you will notice that your right hand is also moving to accommodate the deep breathing. Your rib cage will have expanded, releasing the muscles of your middle back. As you exhale, let the impulse begin with the diaphragm, emptying out the old breath from bottom to top. Continue breathing like this, inhaling and exhaling fully and completely. You will establish a wave-like pattern with the Complete Breath, and you

PHOTO COURTESY OF JUST COMMUNICATIONS

You will establish a wave-like pattern with the Complete Breath, and you will find yourself relaxed and refreshed at the completion of the exercise.

will find yourself relaxed and refreshed at the completion of the exercise.

By observing your breath and making the breath the Point of Concentration rather than your nervousness or the various potential distractions ready to steal your attention away from your objective, you are able to stay present in the moment, conscious of your purpose and of your audience's needs. You also will begin to learn more about how you function under stress. The data which you gather will help you in future presentations.

Sense memory is the tool which brings vividness and life to your presentations, and in combination with breath awareness, your public speaking becomes dynamic and memorable. Try the following exercise: think of a vivid sensory experience in your life. It's important to choose something which affected your senses—touch, sight, sound, taste, or smell—in a particularly intense way. Give yourself time to enter into the memory of this experience, so allow your breath to become diaphragmatic and regular to begin with. Close your eyes. As you re-live the event, you may find that your breath will speed up or slow down in response to re-experiencing the event. Notice this change of breath and notice all other physical changes which occur to you as you reconstruct in as much detail as possible the surroundings, the progression of events, and your reactions to the events. Now, with this re-creation fresh in your body and mind, describe the experience in words. Then act it out without words, being aware of your breath and how your body responded when you thought through the event in your imagination. Take your time.

The immediacy, intensity, and vividness of your non-verbal enactment and verbal encoding is the special personalization which you have to offer your audience. They don't want a dispassionate description of your helicopter ride inside a dormant volcano on a paradise island. They will be moved and will experience the vicarious thrill of the sanctity of that moment only if you allow yourself to be affected by the memory of the event as you are telling it. You may actually find yourself getting chills again and pausing to take in your breath as you speak, because the technique of sense-memory takes your imagination back to the event itself.

Allow yourself to get excited as you speak. Your emotional freedom and commitment to communicating your enthusiasm about your subject will in turn excite your audience. But remember that the point is honesty. If you didn't feel any intensity of response and you overdo, your audience is likely to sense your insincerity. If you feel any inhibition in allowing yourself to be emotional and expressive, don't despair. That's what the next chapter addresses.

Chapter 5

Freedom In Expression

One of my students who profited most from my *Professional A.C.T.* course was also the one who seemed initially to be the most inhibited and shut-down. He was a lawyer who committed an hour and a half every week in order to attend the class, so I know that he was motivated. But he seemed to be very passive, sitting silently with arms and legs crossed, expressing non-verbally that he didn't want to disclose himself or be touched in any way. I thought he was belligerent at first, but soon discovered through his very carefully considered and phrased questions and the frequency of his inquiries how much he wished to learn and how much he was willing to commit himself to the process. He just didn't know the emotional language, or else he had forgotten how to use it.

This student chose as his "vivid sensory experience" an event in his office when he gave his secretary an important document to type and discovered that she had made a mistake. This was, for him, a vivid sensory experience. What a bleak, emotionally two-dimensional life he must have led! Or perhaps he felt the need to protect all intensely personal or emotional experiences from public scrutiny.

When people have been hurt a lot and have experienced profound suffering, many often choose to paralyze themselves with drugs or alcohol, or to numb themselves by turning off emotionally. When asked to relate the story of their suffering, they dispassionately recite the events leading to their pain. To express the hurt, and thereby allow themselves to feel any vestige of that pain is impossible for them. The leather hide which protects them from being hurt again also prohibits them from giving free expression to their emotional lives.

Often this emotional paralysis is given physical expression in a torso which appears to be locked and immovable. The breath is often shallow and unconsciously held. The rigid physical exterior is a fortress beyond which nothing can intrude to add further pain to an already unbearable sadness. The price which is paid for this impenetrable security system is that one fends off not only that which may hurt but also those strokes and balms which could soothe and heal. One forgoes whatever comfort might be provided through the creation in words, art, dance, or music of a crystallization of the grief which has been endured.

Sometimes people avoid being emotional or expressive because they feel that they will appear foolish or weak. Remember my first acting teacher telling me that "if you are willing to be foolish, you will never look like a fool." Pretentiousness is usually a disguise for foolishness. Pretending to be that which you are not is apt to get you into trouble sooner or later. But sincerely expressing your opinions and responses in a simple and straightforward way with commitment and tenacity will never be misinterpreted as foolishness. In fact, far from ridiculing someone for being expressive and vulnerable, people usually sympathize and feel a personal connection and gratitude to a speaker who takes the risk of making an emotional commitment to what he is saying.

People usually feel a personal connection and gratitude to a speaker who takes the risk of making an emotional commitment to what he is saying.

One does not need to be an actor in order to present an exciting and involving public address. One does not need to "ham it up" in order to make a point sincerely and expressively in a way which is unique to oneself. What is necessary is the willingness to be generous—to share yourself with your audience, not just the information which you have gathered and interpreted, but your own personality and individual point of view, enriched by your life experiences, wit, warmth, and charm.

In a Profile of Jesse Jackson by Marshall Frady for the Feb. 3, 1992 edition of *The New Yorker,* Reverend Jackson talks about his speaking style:

> Lot of people say, you know, 'He's a great speaker.' Well, speaking is a result of feeling, of *thinking*—you *thought* of what to say. So when people say, 'He sho does talk good,' ain't just talkin', it's a *brain.* I got a brain that sends messages to my jaw muscles. I be feeling and *thinking* what I'm talking. I work, and work, and work to say that thing right, spin that thing just right, so when people hear it, the—" He blew out a soft whoosh of breath—*whew!*—while yanking himself upright in his seat, wide-eyed, as if from a sudden shock. "It's like that. I struggle hard to conceive it as a *live* thing." He went on about this some while later: "When I first came back home from the seminary, I was asked to speak at church, and my grandmother and some of the older folk came up afterward, 'That was a nice speech, young man, very nice speech.' They meant the words were. Words came out nice. That's what it was, was a speech. But as you go on and begin to really catch hold of it, you start hearing them say, 'Well, now! You spoke to my soul. You burned me this morning.' Got to do more than *speak.* You can get informed listening to a newsman or weatherman. You got to be moving toward the heart of the matter, got to burn people's souls. You got to get *inside* of people. That's where it all is. And you can't get inside of them unless you open *yourself* up to be got inside *of.* Follow what I'm saying? The key to other people's hearts is finding the key to yours. Got to give to receive, got to open up yourself to get inside somebody else."

Whatever the reasons why we fall into the habit of living life in a small way, the manifestation of that decision is visible in our bodies, in our voices, and in our apparent lack of vulnerability. A physical approach to the problem is through breath awareness and a program of exercise. The relaxation which one experiences after physical exertion and the ease which accompanies the relaxed inhalation and exhalation of the breath clears away excess tension so that the body and voice can be expressive. If I'm working with someone who is stiff and breathing shallowly, I might have him do sit-ups or run in place until he is panting and then instruct him to begin to speak. While the sweat is dripping off his brow, and he is gasping for breath, he is not preoccupied with maintaining an immovable exterior. It's physically impossible. Then he is forced to use his diaphragm while he speaks!

Dancers do extensive barre exercises before they begin to rehearse. Their bodies are warmed-up and limber; tension and tightness are reduced so that they can express the vision of the choreographer free from physical limitations. Singers keep their throats warm and protected from the elements and will do vocal warm-ups before they sing, knowing that their instruments need that exercise in order to produce the best sound.

No matter how fascinating your speech may be, and no matter how poised you appear, standing in front of a group, your communication efforts are lost if you are not heard. Likewise, it will be easier to listen to you, and people will be more receptive to you if your voice is vigorous, strong, and pleasing to listen to. So take the time to warm up your voice. Not only will you prepare yourself vocally by warming up, but you will also be energizing yourself generally because the diaphragm and the breath will be working for you.

I vocalize in the car on the way to a performance. The enclosed space feels protected, so I can sound just as silly as I please. I think of myself as a sound machine as I do these exercises, letting the diaphragm be my motor and the breath my fuel.

Sit up and out of your hip joints, or stand tall, with your feet about the distance of your shoulders apart. Let your neck be easy and free of tension. Notice your breath. Yawn and relax more. Do

PHOTO COURTESY OF JUST COMMUNICATIONS

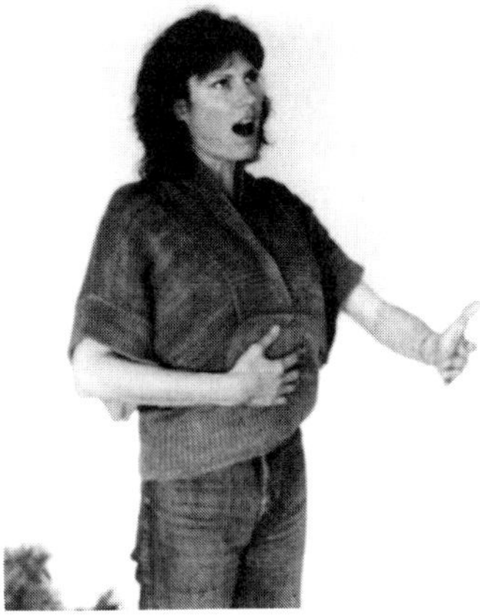

People will be more receptive to you if your voice is vigorous, strong, and pleasing to listen to. So take the time to warm up your voice.

some neck turns (if you're not driving!), first bringing your right ear to your right shoulder and holding it there for about ten seconds. Remember to continue to breathe through your nose. Then bring your left ear to your left shoulder and hold. Bring your chin to the hollow of your chest and hold, and then let your head stretch back to a comfortable position and hold. Look over your right shoulder and hold, and then look over your left shoulder and hold. Now come easily back to center. These neck turns are gentler and safer than neck rolls, which can be too intense for some people, and they are just as effective in releasing neck and throat tension.

Now take an easy, fairly low pitch which you can sustain and "sing" the nonsense sounds "Mah, Meh, Mee, Meh, Mah, Maw, Moo, Maw." Hum each "M" sound before you go on to the vowel, hearing the sound resonate inside your head. The bones and cavities in your head are what the sound bounces off of and fills up making the sound sonorous and rich. Feel the vibrations buzzing in your head as you hum and then relax your jaw to allow the open vowel sound to emerge. You can then take a pitch a bit higher and repeat the same sounds up and down the scale to limber up your voice. Do this part of the exercise slowly and easily.

After you feel your voice resonating in your head, and your throat is becoming warm and relaxed, use the same sequence of vowel sounds but, starting with the beginning of the alphabet, quickly explode the syllables, starting with "B," "Bah, Beh, Bee, Beh, Bah, Baw, Boo, Baw," then "C," "Cah, Ceh, Cee, Ceh, Cah, Caw, Coo, Caw," and on through all the consonants of the alphabet. You can work up speed to increase your breath support, taking in a deep breath at the beginning and continuing with a steady exhalation through the exercise until you need to take in more breath. How far do you get before you need more air? Don't force yourself, but realize the importance of good breath support. Some speakers have a tendency to hyperventilate because they are taking too many quick breaths and not using up all the air they take in. Really work your lips in this exercise to free them so that they can articulate clearly and rapidly.

Here is another exercise for breath support. Breathe in deeply through the nose and count:

One and two and
One and two and three and
One and two and three and four and
One and two and three and four and five and
One and two and three and four and five and six and
One and two and three and four and five and six and seven and . . .

Continue as long as you can on one breath. Then breathe in again and repeat the exercise.

You want your voice to be powerful, strong, and supported. This is a good exercise to work on those qualities. Using the nonsense series of sounds *Mah Nah Lah Thah Vah Zah,* change the accented syllable, starting with

MAH nah lah thah vah zah
mah NAH lah thah vah zah
mah nah LAH thah vah zah
mah nah lah THAH vah zah
mah nah lah thah VAH zah
mah nah lah thah vah ZAH
MAH NAH LAH THAH VAH ZAH

Really punch the accented syllable and power through the other syllables.

There are endless lists of tongue twisters to use to increase your agility and articulation. Here are some I like, but feel free to use any of your own:

> Red Leather, Yellow Leather, Red Leather, Yellow Leather . . .
> Red Lorry, Yellow Lorry, Red Lorry, Yellow Lorry . . .
> Six Slack Black Knap Sack Straps

Have fun with your vocal exercises and make them an automatic ritual each time before you speak publicly.

The exercise program you choose needs to provide you with a sense of deep relaxation. If you feel more stress as a result of the regimen, keep looking. I recommend Hatha Yoga as taught by an experienced, good teacher. One outcome in the practice of yoga is learning where you hold tension in your body and how you can release that tension. This knowledge will not only help you in public speaking situations, but will be valuable in every area of your life.

My series of hatha postures has been modified over time to include those stretches which my body responds to best. Although my back is very flexible and my "double-jointedness" has always made it easy for me to do extreme back bending and twisting postures with ease and agility, I discovered through sensitively listening to what my body was telling me that those postures were straining my back. Now my morning series of postures, which I also use as a warm-up before a performance, consists of the Solar Salutation, a series of Triangle postures, some balance postures, forward bends, the shoulder stand, plough, abdominal lifts, and the headstand. I supplement these postures with exercises taught to me by a physical therapist which are designed specifically for the back. I add an aerobic workout every other day, running three miles. This is my own routine which I find works best for me right now. From time to time it changes, depending on what I am feeling and hearing from my body. A physical exercise program will give you the ability to listen to your body and know what is good for it.

As you become more attuned to your own body through your exercise program, you will begin to know when you are tightening a muscle group in response to a stressful situation and will be able to let that area consciously relax without having to rely upon drugs or alcohol. You will also experience more ease with your body as an expressive instrument as a result of the exercise program.

It's impossible to be focused on your topic and your delivery if your mind is jammed with chaotic thoughts left over from home, the freeway, or your office.

By the same token, mental relaxation is essential for the public speaker or presenter. It's impossible to be focused on your topic and your delivery if your mind is jammed with chaotic thoughts left over from home, the freeway, or your office. You must cultivate the ability to clear your mind of distractions and let go of anything which does not pertain to your presentation.

This is one of the benefits to be gained from meditation and breath awareness. So sit quietly and bring your attention to the point where your breath enters and leaves your nostrils. Watch the inhalation and exhalation passively, without trying to control the breath. If you have a mantra, let the mantra be there, coming back to it when you realize that you are chasing thoughts left over from your busy life. If you don't have a mantra, you can use the word *One,* saying it silently to yourself again and again as you observe your breath.

The regular practice of meditation will result in your ability to focus your thoughts and concentrate more effectively. It will also give you the ability to rest your mind, clearing it of distracting prattle and the futile reiteration of what you should have said to so-and-so, the list of things you need to pick up at the store on the way home, etc.

For some people, performance itself is a liberation. Many

actors confess to being painfully shy and introverted, yet when they are on the stage, they feel they have been given permission to be totally free and uninhibited. The stage offers them a deliverance from their shy persona to become someone else, free from their own neuroses and complexes.

One of the most popular sessions in the *Professional A.C.T.* was led by a friend of mine who is a mime. He brought to the class his suitcase filled with hats and masks which he had made, and he asked each student to choose a mask to wear. He then set up a scene with a shopkeeper and a customer, with the students playing the roles and wearing the masks.

I found that this class was particularly effective in blasting through preconceived notions of what students thought they were capable of doing in front of an audience. They felt a blissful anonymity while wearing the masks and were free to be more physically expressive than they previously thought possible. The results of the exercise were nearly always eloquent and rich.

You might surprise yourself with your own abandon by rehearsing your presentation once with a Halloween mask or a grocery sack covering your head!

A favorite technique used by one acting teacher I know is to instruct classmates to physically restrain one student while he performs a monologue. Whatever preoccupation there may have been with what to do with his hands, or whether or not he looks impressive in front of the group, etc., becomes secondary to the struggle against the resistance. When the resistance is removed, the meaning and message of the monologue become the primary focus, as they should be.

Visualization is a powerful tool to learn to use. We will talk about it in more detail in Chapter 6, Listening Skills. Many athletes visualize the perfect execution of their event for weeks and months beforehand. Prior to their performance they have a clear mental picture of themselves in minute detail which they mentally replay again and again.

Let this technique work for you by imagining yourself in an empowered state. In other words, see yourself as an effective, energized, expansive, persuasive speaker, confidently approaching the podium, speaking clearly, resonantly, and powerfully, convincing your audience, through your presentation, of your thesis.

Close your eyes, observe your breath, and feel your body relaxed and yet alert. Imagine the warmth and brilliance of the sun washing over your body and your body drinking in the vitality of the rays. Every part of your body is becoming energized by the solar power of the sun. Imagine yourself as you want to appear to others. Commit yourself to the reality of this vision of yourself. See yourself, hear yourself speak, and feel the energy of your body in this empowered state.

Do this many times, as often as you rehearse your presentation so that your visualization of this empowered you is intimately connected with your address. Then when the time comes for your presentation, surrender yourself to this empowered picture of yourself which you have visualized and let this image take over.

The goal of effective communication is to communicate spontaneously and freely through your own unique, individual voice, from your own, personal perspective of the universe. Children disarm us with their ability to cut through any situation with their perceptions and interpretations of reality, unspoiled by pretense or falseness of any kind.

Over the years, many of us lose the ability to be spontaneous and playful because of the fear of disapproval and of being judged. We censor ourselves subconsciously and consciously, weighing carefully what we say before we speak. Oftentimes this judiciousness is necessary, but many creative and vivid ideas get lost in the filtering process. If we are smart, we are able, as adults, to allow ourselves protected times when we are allowed to be totally unrestrained in our thinking and our expression of what is most intensely and uniquely ourselves.

The Sound and Movement Exercise which I used in the early classes served the purpose of coaxing students to be reckless, abandoned, and uncensored. Standing in a circle, one student goes into the center of the group and performs a simple movement over and over again until another student joins the center person in repeating the same movement. When the first student sees that the second student is correctly repeating the movement,

Number 1 steps to the outside again. Then Number 2 lets the movement evolve to a new movement which is then repeated again and again until a third student comes to the center to imitate the movement. After everyone has participated in the Movement exercise, begin the exercise again, adding a nonsense sound to the movement.

People at first feel foolish in the exercise, but when concentration becomes unfocused or they begin to giggle, I instruct them to watch and listen carefully in order to perfectly imitate the leader. Trust in each other develops swiftly, and the students come to the classes knowing that anything goes within the safety of the classroom. They recognize that this is the time for experimentation and taking chances.

Tom Hanks' performance as a thirteen year old boy in the movie, *Big*, was delightful to watch. His commitment was one hundred percent, and he faithfully and truthfully embodied the imagination and energy of adolescence. Allow yourself some safe period of time in a safe atmosphere where you will not feel exposed or intruded upon to vent the inner, playful child within. Be expansive in your expression. See what it feels like to be outrageous and silly. In this way, you will unlock the doors to

PHOTO COURTESY OF BEYNCH PRESS

Be expansive in your expression.
See what it feels like to be outrageous and silly.

your own imagination and inventiveness so that your creative ideas will be more available to you, and you will be more capable of expressing them without censorship.

You can explore your expression of emotion by yourself by taking each of these emotions, or any others which come to you.

Sorrow
Fear
Anger
Joy

Begin small and increase the intensity of each emotion while you are standing still, without movement. Think about the emotion and how that emotion manifests through you. Don't imitate what you observe in other people. This will only appear false and disingenuous. If you have difficulty, think of a time when you felt that particular emotion and reconstruct in your memory the details surrounding that event. The more specific you are in the mental recreation, the more successful you will be in bringing to the surface the memory of that emotion.

Now, use the same emotions with a simple activity, like sweeping the floor. Observe how the action changes depending on the emotion you are feeling at the time. Whenever you get carried away with the emotion, come back to your intention of sweeping the floor, and whenever you become preoccupied with the thorough cleaning of the floor, reintroduce the intense emotion.

There are always times when you feel resistant or unwilling to push yourself beyond familiar territory. Students give themselves away by attempting to distract the teacher with questions or personal observations just at the point when, if they kept going, exploring the new terrain, there might be significant and surprising discoveries. This breakdown point is a difficult hurdle to overcome, but the value in proceeding beyond the limit which you previously drew for yourself is worth the risk and the fear associated with encountering it.

I was cast in a show playing a part which was a stretch for me. I was a self-centered, selfish, vain, snooty woman, and I had to deal with three-inch heels, gloves, a purse, and a flask filled with alcohol. The director gave me lots of new moves and ideas, faster than I could assimilate them, and I was getting very frustrated and angry. I wanted him to slow down and let me work it out slowly, but he continued to press me until I no longer could consciously control the character. It was at this point that I remember the character starting to achieve a life of her own. Up until then I was manipulating her like a puppeteer handles the strings of a marionette. I didn't like being at that breakdown point and feeling the loss of control, but the character grew from the stretch.

Remember: "If you always do what you've always done, you'll always get what you've always got." In the classroom there is an accepting environment where the child within each person is valued, listened to, and encouraged. The result is that enthusiasm, joy, playfulness, wit and inventiveness is nurtured and flourishes.

There is a very effective exercise taken from *The Student Actor's Handbook* by Desrezan called "Body Metaphors" which I adapted for *The Professional A.C.T.* As a group, the students begin to walk randomly about the room. I instruct them to let the various metaphors which I call out to them inform and color the way in which they move. For instance, I say "head in the clouds," "two-faced," or "poker face" and their movements reflect the suggestion of the metaphors. I let them experiment with their movements, encouraging them to expand and exaggerate them to overcome any feelings of inhibition or silliness. I instruct them to speed up or slow down the movements in order to concentrate their focus on their physicalizations and to forget their self-consciousness.

On the next page there are some other metaphors to try:

highbrow	open arms
hawk-eyed	itching to do it
nose out of joint	hang loose
nosey	cold-blooded
tight-lipped	feel it in your bones
stiff upper lip	thin-skinned
tongue-tied	uptight
tail between your legs	pushover
drag your feet	pushy
cheeky	blow-hard
lump in your throat	light-headed
pain in the neck	evil-eyed
shoulder a burden	spineless
bleeding heart	blue-blooded
lily-livered	wide-eyed
butterflies in your stomach	
bright-eyed and bushy-tailed	

It's important with the Body Metaphor exercise not to think about what you are going to do before you do it. Boldly and vividly do what first comes into your mind. The purpose is to give your body and mind a playground for imaginative play. One has to exercise those childlike faculties which have been neglected over the years. I prefer to let my students do these exercises as a group so that they feel more freedom and safety within the group, but you can also work at home individually with beneficial results.

Another exercise with the purpose of freeing the student of physical inhibitions in order to be more physically expressive is adapted from Marjorie Fink Vargas' *Louder Than Words*.

Walk as if:

you know you look sharp
you think you're ugly
you're crossing the stage to get an award
you're with someone you're proud of
you're on your way to a class you hate (a class you love)
you're trying to impress a group of the opposite sex
you want to pass someone but not be seen by him
you're trying to sneak in to a meeting late
you want to annoy the people downstairs
you're late for class but afraid to be caught running down the hall

(Using a static pose, sit as if:)

you're in a boring class
you're having a job interview
you're posing for a portrait
you're having breakfast alone
you're trying to think of a good speech topic
you're in a movie theater watching a spy thriller
you're putting medication on a burn
you're waiting for the dentist
you're in your favorite class
you're dining in an elegant restaurant

Once the body is again accustomed to expressing itself freely and eloquently, turn your attention to your vocal expressiveness. The best material to work with, providing rich language and enormous ideas and images, is Shakespeare. Take a sonnet, like the 29th:

When, in disgrace with Fortune and men's eyes,
I all alone beweep my outcast state,
And trouble deaf heaven with my bootless cries,

And look upon myself and curse my fate,
Wishing me like to one more rich in hope,
Featured like him, like him with friends possessed,
Desiring this man's art, and that man's scope,
With what I most enjoy contented least,
Yet in these thoughts myself almost despising,
Haply I think on thee, and then my state,
Like to the lark at break of day arising
From sullen earth, sings hymns at heaven's gate;
For thy sweet love rememb'red such wealth brings
That then I scorn to change my state with kings.

Work with each word individually, understanding the depth of meaning inherent in the words. Consider the words as if they are filled with all of history's impact upon the ideas which the words embody. It's as if each word is capitalized, and the way your voice intones the word carries with it the meaning and melody of mankind's concept of each idea.

After each word is separately considered and intoned, put them together slowly, thinking as you go of all the meaning which you have attributed to each idea. You may wish to actually sing the sonnet because it may take melody to encompass all the richness which you have discovered within the poetry. As you continue to work with the sonnet, work with the image of a continuous ribbon of energy coming from your mouth. Think of the ribbon originating in your diaphragm, and on the ribbon is written the words of the sonnet.

Let your voice be full and rich. If you have access to a tape recorder, tape yourself. Listen to the strength of your voice. Many times slips and vocal or verbal mistakes occur when you have less energy and diaphragmatic support than necessary. Turn up your volume. You may think you're too loud because you're hearing yourself from inside your own head. But if you're in doubt, err on the side of being too loud. There is no faster way to lose your audience than by being too soft to be heard clearly. If you have the opportunity to rehearse a bit in the space in which you are to speak, ask someone to listen to you from the back of the auditorium and to let you know if you need to speak louder. Get to know how much energy is required of you to produce that much volume.

After all the exercising, practicing, and rehearsing is over, forget all the ingredients which you have carefully put into the exploration of the sonnet and simply "speak the speech." The meaning and intent of the words will still underlie your recitation without the painstaking effort. The same thing is true when you are truly prepared for your presentation. Before the time comes for you to approach the podium, you should not be thinking about how to gesture at some moment, or how to give a particular inflection to your voice on a word. Relax, observe your breath, and focus your mind on this moment in time, trusting that all your rehearsal will come to support and aid you as you approach the podium.

Surrender to the moment. It is under these circumstances when you are supremely prepared and yet relaxed that serendipitous inspiration can come to infuse your message with electricity. You are mentally ready, emotionally loose, and physically relaxed, and your spirit and soul are poised, anticipating your moment to communicate to a listening audience.

Surrender to the moment.

Chapter 6 Listening Skills

While effective public speaking is one goal in the study of communication skills, listening skills are at least as important to develop. Many actors are so accustomed to doing their monologues in auditions that they forget, when they are cast in a play, that receiving communication on stage is just as vital to their performance as transmitting words.

The actor who doesn't listen to the other actors on stage is generally only concerned with the effect he is having on his audience. He has lost sight of the reality of the character and of how that character is interacting with the other characters. What results from this shortsightedness is that the audience is pulled out of the reality of the play. We may notice the beautiful voice or the fine figure of the actor, but we have lost sight of the meaning of the dialogue.

A preoccupation with what you have to say is selfish and self-centered. What you say must always be connected to the person you are talking to, responding to what they have said to you. Therefore you must listen carefully, not only to the words, but also to the subtext, the body language and other non-verbal clues which tell you about the underlying views and opinions of the other person and how passionately they are held.

I once received a phone call from a movie producer who had

heard about me and wanted me to come to his "office" for an audition. I asked about the production he was working on and tried to get details about the project. It didn't take long to figure out that the producer was disreputable, that the script was shoddy, that his "office" was his apartment, and that there was no financing for the project. Although he was very persistent, I knew that this was not an audition I should go to, and later my suspicions were confirmed by the other actors in the community who were less discriminating about the auditions they went to.

You can let other people know that you are sympathetic to what they have to say before you say a word by the body language and eye contact you establish while listening to them. You can communicate non-verbally that you understand them and that you are on their side, even if you wish to persuade them of another point of view. Without interrupting you can nod your head or indicate with an affirmative sound or a spoken "yes" that you are following them and want them to continue. By maintaining eye contact, even when their eyes wander, you let them know that you are concentrating on their message. And by letting your body be open to the speaker and even inclining physically toward him, you signal that you are attentive to him.

It helps to know as much as possible about the personal history of your audience. Not only can you win them over by mentioning something about their community or cultural heritage or alma mater, but these details will also give you valuable clues about them. What kind of economic background do they come from? How much education do they have? You don't want to alienate someone with a high school education by appearing too intellectual and condescending. Ask yourself what values are important to them. The more you know about what you do and don't have in common, the better off you'll be. Whatever the differences are, you'll be prepared to bridge the boundaries with what you have in common.

Understanding cultural differences can clarify what can otherwise lead to misunderstandings. For instance, my father, a retired businessman who operated a very successful tire and appliance store through many years of hard work, sacrifice and determination, had difficulty in understanding the values and motivating drive of the local Hawaiian people when he and my mother moved to the rural island of Kauai. While he was attacking the jungle of overgrown brush in the valley of his property, clearing it in order to have an unobstructed view of the waterfall from the house, local kids were skipping classes at the junior college to enjoy the sun and surf. It isn't that the local students are irresponsible, but that their cultural values are vastly different from my father's, which are heavily influenced by the Great Depression which his family struggled through. I'm sure that more than one of his neighbors thought my father's machete labor was obsessive and a waste of time and labor.

As human beings and inhabitants of the same planet, we all have some values and goals in common which we can identify. We all want to feel safe in our homes and neighborhoods. We all want clean air to breathe and nutritious food to eat and pure water to drink. We want to be free to pursue whatever careers will bring us a sense of personal fulfillment and sufficient income to buy the things we need and want.

As human beings and inhabitants of the same planet, we all have some values and goals in common which we can identify.

Whatever the cultural or economic differences you may recognize between yourself and your audience, you should identify the common desires and experiences you share and the common goals and commitments you work toward. Come back to these fundamentals when you sense that what your audience wants is in conflict with what you want. Keep these areas of convergence in mind. It is your task to see how you can get what you want while, at the same time, satisfying the desires of your audience.

This concept called *Influencing With Integrity* is the subject of a powerful book by the same title written by Genie Laborde. The idea of satisfying your needs and the needs of the other person in a perfect fit is called "dovetailing." Beautifully crafted furniture features joints which fit together. The interlocking wood strengthens the seam without using nails or screws. Your goal in persuasive communication should be to find a way of interlocking views from both sides to come up with a unified and strong synthesis of ideas which leaves neither side feeling disenfranchised.

You need to be cognizant of what options, objectives, personal histories, and congruencies you share with your audience. Instead of focusing on the gap separating them from you, see yourself as someone whose defining characteristics overlap with your audience's profile in crucial ways. These areas of overlap may not be discernible at first glance, but you can learn to widen your focus in order to see and experience commonalities rather than divergences.

The investigation of common goals and motivating desires is simplified by the technique of "Chunking." The students in *The Professional A.C.T.* practice this technique in the following exercise, where the aim is to reply to a given word with a logically related word that is more specific, less specific, or equally specific.

In a circle, one person starts with a word (a noun) followed by one of three commands: "chunk up," "chunk down," or "chunk sideways." For instance, if one person says, "Kayak; chunk up," the next person might answer, "Boats" (an kayak is a specific example of the larger general category of boats). The command to "chunk sideways" from "Boats" might lead to "Cars" (boats and cars both belong to the category, "transportation"). Then the command to "chunk down" from "Cars" could lead to the response, "Volkswagen" (a specific type of car).

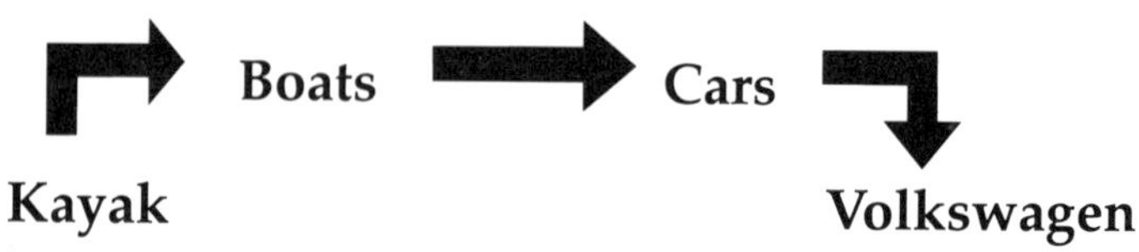

You will gain skill through the "chunking" exercise in drawing connections between characteristics shared by your audience and yourself. By "chunking up" you will arrive at basic values, common goals, and outcomes which you share with your audience.

Sometimes when you are in a problem-solving situation, you can get stuck thinking of the problem from only your own perspective and preclude finding a creative solution which could satisfy your needs while at the same time pleasing the other people involved. Getting used to the ability to "chunk up, down, and sideways" gives you practice in easily changing the context of your thoughts about the problem at hand.

How many times have you worked on a puzzle or problem for hours without finding any solution and then put it side for a while in frustration only to find that when you came back to it, the solution was immediately apparent? Going away from the problem or approaching it from another point of view seems to unjam our thought processes enough to get a different handle on the situation.

Instead of becoming entrenched and stubbornly determined that only one path will lead to a particular outcome, loosen up your parameters by "chunking down" to the underlying common motivations and "chunking up" to those goals which are shared. Expand your tunnel-vision thought from focusing on the content of the particular facts and details to discovering a new context where the possibility of finding creative and mutually satisfying solutions becomes greater.

It is particularly important to be able to listen carefully to the other person when you are involved in a discussion in which the participants are emotionally involved and passionately and tenaciously defending their point of view. Many times it is during these volatile confrontations that listening stops, and each participant becomes preoccupied with defending himself, precluding understanding or a synthesis of opinions. We tend to lose sight of the goal of arriving at a meeting of minds and get stuck vehemently attempting to reiterate our own position. While this may be conducive to colorful cocktail party verbal pyrotechnics, it is not a particularly advisable method to use if you want to reach a mutually satisfying outcome.

The best director and conversationalist I know is also my partner in life. I admire his ability to win others over to his way of thinking. He always begins by subtly praising the strengths of the other person, acknowledging with acceptance and affirmation their most vigorously held beliefs. It appears at first as if he is championing the other person's point of view. He then manages to dovetail his own thesis to this very argument, pointing out how his own argument solves the problem or resolves the conflict more effectively. He manages to diffuse the opponent's anger by first complimenting him for whatever strengths his argument holds so that he becomes receptive. And then he introduces his own persuasive solution to his audience. The other person doesn't feel the need to defend because he has already been praised for his wisdom and been applauded for his motivations. By establishing oneself as an advocate, you can offer a better solution which can be accepted without any loss of self-respect to either side.

Try to view communication as a game like volleyball where the goal is to keep the ball in the air as long as possible. Players on both sides of the net are after the same goal, not opposing each other but working with the other team players to achieve the same goal.

Listen to what is being communicated to you. Try to discover the intention of the person talking to you and then see how your own intention can dovetail with your partner's. In this way, you achieve your outcome without thwarting the purpose of your listener.

Try to view communication as a game like volleyball where the goal is to keep the ball in the air as long as possible.

Neurolinguistics is a fascinating study of the way people communicate with each other. This science has developed through the observation of effective communicators. By familiarizing yourself with some of the techniques and patterns discovered in the field of Neurolinguistics, you can add to your own expertise and knowledge of successful communication.

John Grinder and Richard Bandler have written several books about Neurolinguistics which present the techniques they have taught in their workshops. I strongly recommend any of their books for those who are interested in Neurolinguistics. They developed their work by observing Milton Erickson and his use of hypnosis and Virginia Satir's methods in family counseling. Grinder and Bandler observed the processes that the brain uses. By changing these processes, dramatic personal changes can take place. NLP demystifies the study of psychology because, according to Bandler and Grinder, the brain does what it is told to do, not necessarily what you want it to do. So the trick is to learn how to tell the brain to do what you want.

Instead of analyzing behavior with questions such as "What was your childhood like?" or "Describe your relationship with your mother," the method of Neurolinguistics moves beyond content. The process is based not on what made you the way you are, but on how you can effect change now. Therefore, Neurolinguistics is an educational process which assumes that people aren't "broken." They work perfectly according to how they have been taught. We can teach ourselves to work differently by teaching ourselves new information.

One of the most important things I've learned through reading Bandler and Grinder's books is that "the meaning of communication is in the response it elicits." Think about a time when you had a discussion with someone, and the other person misunderstood what you said. It may have resulted in hurt feelings, and yet you felt that you were not at fault. But the outcome of the communication was that *what was perceived* caused misunderstanding. A message was received; unfortunately, it was not the message you may have intended to transmit. In order to judge whether you communicated effectively, you must ask: what message has been received? What is the response to my message?

If you have a son who wants to watch television all morning on Saturday, and who has the habit of responding negatively to any suggestions from you, you probably won't be successful in getting him to go outside to play if you suggest, "Honey, why don't you go outside and ride your bike for a while." You might get the response you are seeking if you were to say instead, "I thought I'd watch t.v. with you this morning, and we can talk about what we've seen afterward." You didn't verbally say that you wanted him to go outside, but the effect of your words was what you wanted. What you are doing is noticing the way the other person's brain works and then adjusting your communication in order to arrive at the outcome you desire.

One of the first ways that you can develop rapport with another person is through observing breathing. Match your breath to his pattern of breathing, inhaling and exhaling with him. This is a very simple and subtle way of profoundly affecting the dynamics between people. The breath is fundamental to us all. Unconsciously, we feel an alliance with another person who is taking in breath with the same depth and rhythm as our own. Try this whenever you have the opportunity and observe the results!

Another easy way of gaining rapport is by matching the tone of voice and vocal level of the person to whom you are talking. If you are talking to someone who has a low voice and slow delivery, bring your own voice down a little and slow yourself down. Otherwise, you may appear aggressive or agitated even if you aren't. On the other hand, if you are talking to someone who talks forcefully and who projects easily and boldly, and if your own voice is low and your pace is slow, the person to whom you're talking might become impatient with you, perceiving you as a little depressed or lazy.

Communication does not only happen through the use of our auditory channel, even though language is, for most of us, appreciated primarily through sound. But many people are more visually or kinesthetically oriented; they understand more completely and learn more efficiently when they are able to look at a picture or touch an object.

The beauty of the Grand Canyon must be seen by your own eyes to be appreciated. Even a camera doesn't do justice to its grandeur. A verbal description of the experience of a hot tub in a backyard overlooking a golf course in the middle of winter cannot encompass the kinesthetic experience of the event! Have you noticed how some people get confused by looking at maps while other people need to have instructions diagrammed in order to understand how to get someplace?

After a show has opened and the cast has had a couple of days off, the stage manager often calls for a line run-through where the cast recites the lines very quickly without actually moving about on the stage in order to refresh their memory of the text. Some actors remember their lines as they appear on the printed page. When they forget a line, they actually locate that line in their visual memory, as if the page were being projected on a screen before their eyes. These people are "visual."

During these line run-throughs, I must concentrate on establishing the memory of the movements which I execute while I deliver the lines on stage. I am incapable of totally divorcing the text from the kinesthetic representation of the speech through my physicalization of the character. This is a clue that I am more "kinesthetic" than "verbal" or "visual."

Knowing which channel—visual, auditory, or kinesthetic—a person is most comfortable and fluent with can be almost as important as knowing what language is being spoken. For instance, if you were talking about finances and quoting figures and percentages to someone who is visually oriented, you would want to be liberal with your use of visual aids, using pie charts, bar graphs, and colors to define and clarify the points you were making. If you were a decorator trying to please your kinesthetic client with ideas for the renovation of her home, you would do

Visual

Auditory

Kinesthetic

PHOTO COURTESY OF JUST COMMUNICATIONS

well to offer fabric swatches and samples of the polished woods and lacquers you intend to use to create your effects.

The language you choose to communicate with another person can be deliberately chosen on the basis of what that person will most easily understand. A visual person will tend to use verbs like "envision," "color," "see," "show," "draw," etc., while an auditory person would prefer using expressions like "sound her out," "listen to this," "hear me out," etc. Kinesthetic people will say, "It feels like . . .", or "are you in touch with . . ." or "my gut reaction is . . ." etc.

In addition to the use of language as an indicator of the channel of preference, the eyes also offer clues as to whether a person is more visual, auditory, or kinesthetic. Neurolinguists have discovered that by studying eye accessing signals we can discover the channel of preference for any individual.

Visual people access information which they have stored in memory by looking up or defocusing center. When they are trying to remember they will actually turn their eyes up, as if visually seeing the picture of the event above them. Auditory people will access information as if they are reading the information in front of them from left to right, and kinesthetic people will retrieve memories or information by looking down and to the right. By observing the eye accessing cues, you can discover whether a person is more visual, auditory, or kinesthetic.

If you can adapt your own language using this knowledge of Neurolinguistics, you will be more easily understood by other people because you will be "speaking their language."

You can also help to achieve a level of rapport with other people by physically mirroring that person. Have you noticed how couples or friends will oftentimes copy the posture of each other at parties or in restaurants? If one person leans in and puts his elbows on the table with one arm lying on top of the other, how long does it take before the companion does the same?

Try consciously, but subtly, to mirror the posture of the person with whom you are communicating when you are sitting listening to him. If your client is sitting on the sofa, leaning on one arm with legs crossed, slowly and subtly do the same. Then, when you sense that you have achieved a level of rapport with

PHOTO COURTESY OF JUST COMMUNICATIONS

Try consciously, but subtly, to mirror the posture of the person with whom you are communicating.

the client, try this experiment: change your posture and see if the client mirrors you! If so, the chances are that you have achieved rapport with him and that you can proceed to a consensus about the issue at hand. You will find that the client has unconsciously given you the signal that he is ready to concede your point of view.

Ideally, of course, you should have the ability to communicate through the visual, auditory, and kinesthetic channels with equal ease. This flexibility gives you the freedom to talk to and understand everyone easily using their channel of preference. You are then able to consciously determine what kind of language to use depending on the situation and the people with whom youe are negotiating. And the more you practice your communication skills, the more adept you will become in exercising your abilities effortlessly and effectively.

You can use the insight you gain from the study of Neurolinguistics to increase your own effectiveness and self-confidence in particular situations. For instance, if you are working on a presentation and you wish to enhance your preparation for the event, spend some time before each of your rehearsals visualizing, hearing yourself deliver your speech, or imagining the sensations of your body as you present your speech in a powerful, persuasive, and energized way.

My yoga instructor demonstrated the effectiveness of this technique using the difficult posture of the handstand, which I was unable to do and was fearful of even attempting. He instructed the group to visualize ourselves doing the handstand and then to write down what we saw. I saw myself executing a good handstand with columns of light on either side of me which seemed to support me. When he instructed us to imagine performing the handstand while concentrating on the auditory channel, all I could hear were disapproving and disbelieving voices saying that I wasn't coordinated enough to do it.

But when he instructed us to kinesthetically approach the handstand in our imagination, all my fears were transformed into the physical sensation which I associate with carnival rides, which both terrify and delight me. I could tell that, while the visual channel had provided me with a positive, capable, and safe image of myself performing the handstand, my kinesthetic channel had changed my trepidation to excitement and childlike joy in the body rush of a carnival ride. From that moment on I've enjoyed the ability of doing a good handstand without any fear!

The ability to visualize is something you can develop.

The ability to visualize is something you can develop, and it can be a great help to you as you prepare to give a talk or a presentation in front of a group of people. Although visualization techniques have become increasingly popular in recent years, it is a practice which is ancient. In religious traditions, it is believed that images which are held in the mind have the power to affect the physical universe and that thoughts can change the material world. For example, the religious supplicant might hold the image of a sacred fertility god in his mind with the belief and expectation that the energy of that image is transmitted to him. In the practice of Tantric yoga, the yogi mentally projects the image to various chakras to free the energy which is located there. In the Christian communion service, the minister asks the parishioners to accept the bread and wine as the body and blood of Christ as they visualize the Last Supper. The Egyptian followers of Hermes believe that, by holding the image of the healing god, they will receive the benefits of good health.

Robert Ornstein, a research psychologist at the University of California, believes that it is possible to strengthen the right hemisphere of the brain, which is associated with intuitive abilities and with the ability to visualize, by viewing geometric forms, learning crafts, and paying attention to your dreams. Keeping a dream journal, and recording all that you remember of your dreams, seems to increase the ability to remember dreams.

There are two kinds of visualization: receptive visualization and programmed visualization. One of the most famous examples of receptive visualization occurred when Kekule, a 19th century chemist, had a dream image of a snake with its tail in its mouth from which Kekule derived his image of the benzene ring. In his Memorial Lecture of 1898, Kekule describes the vision:

> I was sitting, writing at my text-book; but the work did not progress; my thoughts were elsewhere. I turned my chair to the fire and dozed. Again the atoms were gambolling before my eyes. This time the smaller groups kept modestly in the background. My mental eye, rendered more acute by repeated visions of the kind, could now distinguish larger structures, of manifold conformation: long rows, sometimes more closely fitted together; all twining and twisting in snake-like motion. But look! What was that? One of the snakes had seized hold of its own tail, and the form whirled mockingly before my eyes. As if by a flash of lightning I awoke; and this time also I spent the rest of the night in working out the consequences of the hypothesis.
>
> Let us learn to dream, gentlemen, then perhaps we shall find the truth.

Programmed visualization is a way of intentionally creating a situation where you bring yourself into a receptive alpha level, where your subconscious is more susceptible to suggestion.

It takes some of us practice to increase our ability to visualize vividly and productively. So try this exercise: find a quiet space and consciously decide that for the next few minutes you are going to put aside your preoccupations and concerns. Relax your body by systematically tensing and releasing each part of your body, starting with your feet and working your way up to your head. You may notice that your neck and face, particularly around your eyes and jaw, hold the most residual tension, so spend a little extra time consciously relaxing these areas. Now bring your attention to your breath, noticing your breath as you inhale and exhale at the point where the air enters and leaves your nostrils. When you notice that your mind is wandering, gently bring your attention back to your breath. You don't have to follow each thought as it passes through your mind. Just let it go. Then bring your attention to a clear image of something which you wish to manifest. For instance, you may wish to visualize yourself standing poised and confident on the stage, behind the podium, speaking easily and enthusiastically to the group before you. Do this regularly, two or three times a day, and invest your vision with energy until it becomes, in your mind, a reality. Be sincere. Know that this vision is what you want and that you are creating it by visualizing it in your mind.

The mind is a very powerful tool. When you create something, it begins in thought. So it is important to make your images the ones that you want to manifest in your life. Likewise, the words you speak have potential energy. So it's important to speak using words which are positive and consistent with your vision. It isn't necessary to believe in any power outside of yourself when you visualize. This is an enormous and wonderful potential that we human beings all possess.

By visualizing we are creating a pattern which our subconscious then works on, so the more often we visualize, the more practice the subconscious has to go over the pattern or map. You

When we create something, it begins in thought. So it is important to make your images the ones that you want to manifest in your life.

can get into the habit of visualizing before you go to bed at night or first thing in the morning, before you get out of bed. At these times you are most relaxed and your subconscious is in a receptive state.

We attract to us that which we mentally project, so by visualizing strongly and sincerely, we create a receptive field for those things which we are mentally creating. When I was a child I made a list of everything I wanted to achieve in the coming year. I forgot about the list and found it when I cleaned out my desk years later. Virtually everything which I had written down I had achieved. Ever since then I make a special effort to write down what I want to achieve before the new year begins. I knew that I had to really want everything on my list. There was no room for shyness or ambivalence. If you have some deep-seated feeling that you don't deserve what you want, that will interfere with your ability to clearly visualize yourself having achieved your desire. It's important that you have a strong desire to achieve your vision, a strong belief in your ability to have that vision, and a willingness to have it.

Verbal affirmations are also helpful in aiding your visualizations. Putting into words what you want is a way of committing yourself to it. So state what you wish to manifest in a positive way in the present tense, as if you've already accomplished your vision. An example might be "I am poised, confident and enthusiastic as I speak to these people before me." Make the statements short and use strong language. You'll be able to remember the affirmation more easily throughout the day, and you can even use your visualization and affirmation as a way of clearing your mind and energizing yourself during the day.

Don't worry if your first attempts at visualization are unclear or if you feel that you are sensing the "visualization" more than actually seeing a picture before your eyes. Just get a feeling for the sensations that you are having as you "visualize." Recognize that you aren't resisting your present condition by visualizing something unmanifest and by stating something unattained as being presently true. You are programming yourself, like a computer, knowing that what you are feeding into your brain manifests in the future. If you visualize or word your affirmation in the future, you will be removed from the realization. Program yourself for right now! "I relish this opportunity to speak to these friendly people, and I share with them my knowledge easily and effortlessly."

Chapter 7

Stagefright

I was astonished and curiously comforted when I read that stagefright is at the top of most people's list of "The Things I Fear The Most." It is an affliction suffered by seasoned, extremely gifted, and famous performers as well as non-theater professionals who occasionally present talks to their peers. So when I decided a few years ago that I was going to confront my own stagefright and overcome it, I discovered that I was not alone.

I had been a professional actress for ten years, and although I experienced nervousness before shows and anxiety about my talent when I first acted professionally, I only recently discovered that there were occasions when, in the middle of a run of a show, I found myself in the wings preparing for my entrance thinking, "What happens if I can't remember what I'm supposed to do in the middle of my scene?!"

There was absolutely no rational explanation for my fear. I was adequately rehearsed, I felt confident and successful in my interpretation of my role, and the two other actors in the play were terrific, seasoned actors with whom I loved performing. I don't know why I suddenly became prone to stagefright or what made me capable of making my entrance anyway and doing the show that night just as competently as on any other night. But since then, there have been other occasions when the anxiety which paralyzes many other people before speaking and performing publicly also grips me.

Some time after this first experience, I started to sing solos in my church choir with some regularity. I would have to sing a line or two or maybe a short verse in a choral piece. I was often cast in musical comedies in which I sang many solo numbers. I really loved to sing in front of an audience when I was playing a character within the context of a theater piece. But I was always terrified whenever I had to sing a solo in church. This seemed vastly different to me because I wasn't camouflaged behind the mask of a character. When I refused to sing at my sister's wedding, I was roundly criticized for my apparently willful behavior. After all, I am a professional actress!

Then my closest friend, Linda, a professional singer who also sang in the church choir, asked me to work with her on two Mendelssohn duets to sing at church. I accepted the challenge, flattered that she wanted me to sing with her and excited at the prospect, knowing that our voices would blend beautifully together. I decided that I would use this occasion as a laboratory for confronting my stagefright.

Linda had been diagnosed with ovarian cancer nine months before. Already she looked as if she were several months pregnant, her body swollen from the malignancy. I knew that this would be my last opportunity to sing with her.

I realized that my initial fear of performing onstage years earlier had eventually faded as I became confident of my ability as an actress. My love of theater and performing and the discovery that the audience was attracted to me onstage, and that I could communicate something of value to them, became a stronger motivation for performing than was the deterrent of fear. Objectively, I knew that I could sing well, and I trusted that I could find deliverance from this stagefright as I increased the number of opportunities of confronting the fear of singing.

While I knew that performing in a play or musical requires plenty of rehearsal before going in front of an audience, I never felt that I was well-rehearsed when I sang solos in church. I settled for the limited time allotted for the rehearsal of my song with the choir at choir rehearsal plus some time alone at my piano at home. But for these duets, I worked extensively both with Linda and alone with a tape recorder, until I was intimately familiar with every particle of the music and every nuance of my voice and hers.

I took copious notes investigating my fear, writing down anything that seemed to be meaningful in my confrontation with stagefright. It was as if I were arming myself against this insidiously debilitating menace to my self-confidence and my career. All the while, my battle with stagefright was put into stunning perspective by of Linda's condition. The assault of the cancer on her body was a reality which could not be ignored. And yet, far from diminishing her energy and enthusiasm for life, it seemed as if, in her last year, she was more than ever intensely alive, vibrant, and full. By being close to her, my life was likewise intensified. To allow stagefright to diminish my potential or limit my life and work in any way was a waste which I could no longer tolerate.

I was nervous when the time came for our performance of the first duet, but my nervousness was an exhilaration which I was used to in performing onstage. It seemed to enhance my singing. The music was soaringly beautiful, and the blend of our voices was achingly expressive and rich, as the tape of the service proves to me. I listen to it often for inspiration before a performance. We were never able to perform the second of the duets because Linda's strength quickly ebbed after this, her last, public performance.

> ***The first step in dealing with stagefright is to acknowledge its presence.***

Fear, uninvestigated and unexposed, becomes a monster which becomes more powerful as the victim becomes more and more paralyzed. The first step in dealing with stagefright is to acknowledge its presence and ask yourself what you are afraid of.

Are you afraid that you will make a mistake and earn the disapproval of yourself and your audience? Anytime you speak before a group of people you may feel you will make a fool of yourself and ruin your reputation and disappoint yourself. We always want to make the best impression we possibly can and live up to the best expectations we have for ourselves. This is a heavy burden of responsibility to carry on our shoulders, and the magnitude of the demand for the perfect performance is so great that we may capitulate to being less than we are capable of as a way of saying, "Hey, no contest!" Since there is always the possibility of making a mistake, why try? Or if we can summon up the courage to take the plunge, each moment is spent anticipating and dreading the next moment in which we may commit the stupid blunder.

On the other hand, some suffer from the equally debilitating stagefright caused by the fear of success. Being invisible or mediocre brings with it the comfort of no expectations. If we are boundlessly wonderful and brilliant, then we will have set a standard for ourselves which the public will expect in the future and which we will have to acknowledge as a standard of excellence for ourselves. Excellence sometimes inspires jealousy in others, and we may not feel comfortable putting ourselves in a competitive environment where, once we have shown how good we can be, there will be the expectation of excellence to fulfill in the future.

In Susan Faludi's article, "Speak For Yourself," published in the *Hers* column of *The New York Times Magazine*, Jan. 26, 1992, she explores her belief that women have even more reason to be fearful of the podium than men. She describes how women are conditioned by peer pressure to be silent:

> . . . we kept our eyes glued to the floor during class discussion. Partly this was shyness, a genderless condition. But it was a condition reinforced by daily gendered reminders—we saw what happened to the girls who argued in class. The boys called them "bitches," and they sat home Saturday nights. Popular girls raised their voices only at pep squad.

As recently as the 19th century in the United States, women were not allowed to speak in public places, so women like Harriet Beecher Stowe, who felt the necessity of speaking out against slavery, expressed themselves in their writing instead. Ms. Faludi, after confronting her fear of public speaking, tells us:

> . . . it struck me that in some essential way I hadn't really proved myself a feminist until now. Until you translate personal words on a page into public connections with other people, you aren't really part of a political movement. I hadn't declared my independence until I was willing to declare it out loud. I knew public speaking was important to reform public life—but I hadn't realized the transformative effect it could have on the speaker herself. Women need to be heard not just to change the world, but to change themselves.

Much of the fuel which gives power to fear comes from a lack of the ability to control the event. You can constructively exercise your desire to control by making sure that you have prepared yourself ahead of time as thoroughly as possible. Have all the facts about your subject at hand and have your presentation well-rehearsed. Take care to reduce the variables for stress-producing situations by planning what you will wear, knowing the location of the presentation, how to get there, where to park, etc. Find out where you are on the program, and make sure that the person who introduces you has a suitable introduction prepared. Little things can be very nerve-racking when your adrenaline is already high.

But after you have prepared yourself and your talk, and familiarized yourself with as many of the details as possible, you must let go of your desire to control. It's impossible to be in

---

You can constructively exercise your desire to control by making sure that you have prepared yourself ahead of time as thoroughly as possible.

PHOTO COURTESY OF JUST COMMUNICATIONS

Now the time has come to step out of your own way and let yourself generously give all that you have to offer to your audience.

control of everything, and obsessing about what is out of your hands will only increase your anxiety and fear. Your desire to overmanage the situation will defocus your concentration on what you have to say, which should be your primary concern. Know that you have done everything you can do and that now the time has come to step out of your own way and let yourself generously give all that you have to offer to your audience. A good image to have in mind is letting the material speak for itself, or letting the music sing the song, or letting the playwright speak through you.

I once had the great pleasure of performing the role of Twirler in Jane Martin's *Talking With....* I played a champion baton twirler in a part which was a monologue delivered directly to the audience. I loved playing this role and felt that my work was absolutely true and inspiring. But the knowledge of the perfection of the interpretation sometimes made me frightened before I went onstage, wondering if I would be able to do it again as well as I knew I could. I learned that I had to stop taking responsibility for Twirler. She had an existence apart from me, so my preparation in the wings was to get inside her skin and let her go onstage alone. Whatever she did would be perfect, so I let go of trying to control her. Consequently, there was no reason for me to be afraid.

Every time you make a presentation, or conduct an interview, or are interviewed by someone else, there is tremendous potential in the event. With each additional situation, which in the past may have resulted in stagefright, you have the opportunity of changing your response. As your response changes, you are setting up a whole new set of possible responses for your future self in presentational situations. Tell yourself that right now you have the possibility of speaking with authority and conviction. Know that you are offering something to your audience which will benefit them. The next time you are called upon to speak or present, you will have a powerful memory of a capable, empowered response to an event which previously had the ability to paralyze you. The more you take charge of the possibility of changing your experience, the more your experience will change.

In the treatment of phobics, desensitization has been found to be very effective. The phobic is placed, in a controlled manner, in situations which have triggered anxiety in the past. For instance, if the person is afraid of driving on the freeway, short trips in the car are scheduled, allowing the subject to slowly become accustomed and comfortable to driving again.

Within the context of your frequent rehearsals, use your imagination and visualization techniques to stimulate, in as much detail as possible, the experience of talking or presenting in front of an audience. Before you begin your speech, close your eyes and picture yourself on the stage waiting for your introduction, hearing yourself being introduced, walking up to the podium, and looking out into the audience. Experience all the physical sensations which are stimulated by your imaginary performance. Notice if your throat becomes dry, your hands become clammy, your stomach tense, your knees shaky, etc. In this way, you prepare yourself for these sensations ahead of time so that you are not taken by surprise.

Bandler and Grinder describe a technique which can be used

to deal with stagefright in their book, *Using Your Brain—For A Change*. Visualize yourself sitting in a movie theater watching a movie of yourself in a situation in your past which caused you to be fearful. You are in the projection booth watching yourself sitting in the theater, watching the movie starring yourself, as the movie plays. Then watch the movie rewinding quickly and imagine that there is circus music playing. This is a comic version of the movie you just saw. As it's going in reverse, imagine yourself popping out of the projection booth and popping into the movie. Now visualize the presenting situation in the best of all possible worlds. You are living the event this time, and you are confident and at ease. You enjoy the feeling of competence, and the adrenaline rush is a pleasant sensation for you. You feel empowered by the experience, and you know that what you offer is important and will enhance the lives of those you are talking to.

Right before we stood in front of the congregation to sing, Linda leaned over to me and said, "Look at them. There's so much love out there." She was right. There was. I was so concentrated on my experience, preparing for the duet, that I had lost sight of the audience. We were performing for them.

You are not in opposition to your audience. You are participating with them in this experience. Keep your power and let it work for you to deliver your message to your target. Capitulating to stagefright is a way of giving all of your power into the hands of your audience. You make them much more dangerous than they are. Take an objective look at them. They are on your side. They want to hear a good presentation. They want to like you. They are eager to be entertained and educated by you. You are there to serve them, and they want you to be good. They are there helping you with their eyes and their energy. Let them fuel you. When you think of it in this way, it becomes a pleasure to look into the eyes of individuals in the audience as you speak. Imagine that, with every word you are touching the individual you are looking at. Instead of a general, sweeping gaze, let your eyes rest, in a friendly, direct way, on members of the audience as you randomly speak to one, then another and then another. Each one of those contacts you make is important. You establish a connec-

You are not in opposition to your audience. You are participating with them in this experience.

tion with each person. Expect them to like you, and they probably will.

As Bandler and Grinder write in their book, *Trance-Formations,* " . . . there is some mechanism within people that is capable of doing these things, but it needs to be convinced, it needs to be motivated, it needs to be communicated with, and provided with a context in which to respond." Their book is a good one to read if you are interested in the use of hypnosis as a tool for change.

I sing with the Los Angeles Master Chorale, and we audition every year for the conductor of the Chorale. This was an event which I dreaded when I first auditioned for the group, but since then I've come to anticipate the opportunity of preparing a new aria and presenting it with an accompanist in a semi-formal situation. I was talking to another woman in the Chorale about her audition, and she told me that in past years she never felt that she showed her real abilities in her auditions. She was always very nervous, and on the recommendation of her mother-in-law, a psychologist, she decided to see a hypnotist. She was somewhat skeptical going in to the first session, but figured it was worth a try. The second session was just before the audition, and when she went into the studio to sing, she wasn't sure whether the hypnosis had made a difference or not. But when she started to sing, she was poised and confident and gave her best audition ever. This experience changed her attitude about auditions altogether, because now she has one great experience which she can refer back to, knowing that since she performed beautifully then, she can do it again.

Short of visiting a hypnotist, there are ways that you can effect changes like this on your own. *Trance-Formations* talks about self-hypnosis techniques. The important thing to remember is that you're not tied to your past experiences. Investigate how you respond right now. Know that you have the capability to be brilliant from this day forward. Decide that you want to change, that you want to excel, and put your energy in that direction.

Exaggerate the manifestations of your stagefright by vigorously shaking your hands and legs. Then stop and notice the result of the shaking. If you notice that you hyperventilate when you are nervous, try breathing forcefully and rapidly through your nose while sitting down. Then stop and breathe normally and notice the effect on your system. What do you notice about these physical responses? What might they be contributing to your experience of the event?

Many times when we are nervous, we deny to ourselves and to others that we are anxious. We may feel our body's response to fear and pretend that we are doing fine. Then when we stand up, our weak knees seem hardly capable of supporting our frame, and all we can think about is whether or not we will be able to stand throughout our presentation. A better approach is to own the physical sensations as real and allow them to inform the event and even to enhance the presentation.

Most actors experience a rush of adrenaline before performing, and far from denying the effect of their nerves, they count on this rush to boost their energy to the level they desire for their performance. I seem to have more breath than I know what to do with when I am singing in performance, and if I approach the music denying this manifestation of my nervousness, I will be unable to control the breath from my diaphragm. The consequence is that my voice becomes shaky. However, knowing that I have an overabundance of breath gives me the knowledge I require to prepare a firmer foundation for that breath and provide for it a more powerful, rooted base from my feet all the way up through my body. When I do this, the result is quite magnificent and astonishing. I take my physical response to fear and use it to my own advantage, thereby defusing the power fear might have held over me in future situations!

In order to properly simulate the particular physical responses you have to stagefright, you may need to ask a few friends to allow you to practice on them. Take advantage of as

Take a moment to close your eyes, focus your concentration and observe your breath. Know how you want yourself to look, sound, walk, talk, and be received by your audience. Then give yourself permission to be that embodiment.

PHOTO COURTESY OF JUST COMMUNICATIONS

many opportunities as possible beforehand for "dress rehearsals."

Before you rehearse and before you stand to give your presentation, always take a moment to close your eyes, focus your concentration and observe your breath. During these few moments, allow yourself to hear a kind of self-hypnotic suggestion that you will be, for the next few minutes or half hour, empowered to be as brilliant a communicator as you can imagine yourself to be. Know how you want yourself to look, sound, walk, talk, and be received by your audience. Then give yourself permission to be that embodiment and actively agree to step into the form of your visualization.

It is wise not to fuel already jittery nerves with coffee or caffeinated drinks beforehand. Cut out any sugar, and eat light prior to your presentation. You want your system to be concentrated on communicating your message, not on digesting food.

Open your heart to receive serendipitous inspiration and to generously give yourself to your audience. Allow yourself to be touched. The Prologue in Shakespeare's *Henry V* invokes:

> *"O for a Muse of fire, that would ascend*
> *The brightest heaven of invention . . ."*

Far from dreading an opportunity to speak publicly, in time you will find yourself looking forward to the chance to go before an audience. When you start to relish public speaking and presenting, you will realize the truth in the wisdom of a speaker I once heard who said that "if you're not rejoicing, you're not doing it right!"

Chapter 8

Summary

Actors spend their lifetimes perfecting their technique. They are always in training, and only the amateur and foolish actor would think of going onstage, in front of an audience, without adequate preparation and rehearsal. There are many who have been blessed with a talent for acting or singing. Very few are geniuses, like Jackie Gleason, who in spite of his refusal to rehearse with *The Honeymooners,* was nevertheless brilliant in every episode. The rest of us need to prepare ourselves for performance.

The Professional A.C.T. gives you an idea of how to go about the task of making yourself an effective and expressive communicator. Instead of waiting in dread of the next time you are asked to speak to a group or make a presentation, why not take this challenge. Start right now to prepare yourself for that next opportunity to share with others what you know and what you do best. After all, every day you are presenting yourself to the world. You are representing your firm or yourself and your product with each encounter you make. Begin to implement the skills and techniques you've been reading about while you listen to others and talk to them every day.

Realize that you communicate who you are before you say a word by the way you hold your body and the way you move.

PHOTO COURTESY OF BEYNCH PRESS

Start right now to prepare yourself for that next opportunity of sharing with others what you know and what you do best. After all, every day you are presenting yourself to the world.

Take an objective look at what your body language says about you. If you have a physical habit or problem which you would like to work on, tackle it through a program of physical exercise or body therapy which interests and appeals to you.

Above all, be aware. Notice the messages your body is sending. Is it supporting and enhancing your verbal communication or undermining it? Become sensitive to the kind of energy you draw on to fuel yourself. Consciously work to strengthen your diaphragm so that you have a greater source of power at your command. Let your body be relaxed so that there is an easy and effortless flow of energy. When this is happening, you won't need to worry about gestures—they will be there naturally, when you need them to be, to help illustrate your words.

Develop the ability to have easy and meaningful eye-contact with your audience. The eyes are the mirror of the soul. Your audience wants to know who you are, and they want you to appreciate them as well.

You already have demonstrated that you take initiative. In buying this book, you show that you know that you can add to your knowledge and increase your effectiveness as a public speaker. You are programming yourself to reach a level of greater ability, and you are raising the standards which you have set for yourself. Not only do you expect yourself to excel in your chosen profession, but you also expect yourself to be able to communicate about your profession skillfully and competently without feeling overwhelmed by pressure.

You've learned that the mind influences the body and vice versa. Knowing this, you realize now how your feelings of confidence and assurance affect the physical way you present yourself to the world. You know the benefits which you receive from a personalized course of physical exercise with the goals of fitness, strength, and health. And you appreciate the grace, coordination, and stamina which you derive from your own physical regimen.

You speak in public because you know something which you believe the audience wants to understand. You are there to fill their need. This is your overall objective. For any presentation you define what you want to do and you phrase that in terms of your intention, or objective. Everything you say in some way relates back to this objective. Each moment that you speak, you answer a specific need coming from the audience. In this way, every sentence of your speech becomes a response motivated directly by your audience. You proceed point by point, pearl by pearl, answering their need.

You always have a Point of Concentration to which you can return again and again to center and ground yourself. You are aware of the significance of the easy inhalation and exhalation of your breath, and you pay attention to the profound influence the breath has on each moment you are conscious.

Because you know emotional expressiveness can make your

presentation more vivid and interesting to your audience, you realize the importance of vocally and physically warming up before you speak. You are aware that when the mind is focused and calm, you can concentrate on the presenting situation more completely and can tune out distractions. You develop inner awareness through a form of mental contemplation or meditation combined with breath awareness.

You know how to mentally empower yourself to do your best. There is nothing holding you back from achieving right now what you want to create. You move beyond old expectations and limitations and set new parameters which allow you to excel and expand your range of ability.

You respect the valuable contribution that the "inner child" makes to your presenting and communication skills. You encourage your imagination and select times when you allow yourself to be playful and uninhibited so that you have easy access to your imagination and natural expressiveness whenever you want. You know the wisdom of being able to let go of the need to rigidly control each moment of your presentation, recognizing that when you let go, you allow for serendipitous events to occur.

You respect your audience, or the person you are talking to, so you automatically use the listening skills that you have developed. You know the importance of achieving rapport with other people, and you use your body, eyes, breath, and language to help you do that. You find out as much as you can about your audience's personal history in order to be able to establish common motivations and goals between yourself and your audience.

You have learned that "the meaning of the message is in the response it achieves," so you look for the response to what you say and then adjust your words in order to achieve your objec-

---

There is nothing holding you back from achieving right now what you want to create.

---

tive. Your goal is to satisfy your objective and your audience's objective at the same time, dovetailing your goals in a perfect fit.

You supplement all your preparations with detailed visualizations and strong verbal affirmations, knowing that you are programming yourself for the successful presenting situation. You investigate any feeling of stagefright or anxiety and eliminate the fear of success or failure from your conscious thought. Through a rigorous rehearsal process, you desensitize yourself to many of your manifestations of nerves. You recognize the symptoms you experience as the adrenaline which performers value for giving them energy and life in front of their audience.

When you go to the podium, you begin your life as a successful communicator, free of any fears you had in the past. You create for yourself the successful experience to which you can refer back in the future. You look into the eyes of the audience and recognize in them your allies, helping you create an extraordinary future as a public speaker and expressive communicator.

Bibliography

Acting

Chekhov, Michael. *To The Actor, On the Technique of Acting*. New York: Harper & Row, 1953.

Hagen, Uta. *Respect For Acting*. New York: Macmillan Publishing Co., Inc., 1973.

Lewis, Robert. *Advice to the Players*. New York: Harper & Row, 1980.

McGaw, Charles. *Acting Is Believing*. New York: Holt, Rinehart and Winston, Inc., 1976.

Shurtleff, Michael. *Audition*. New York: Walker & Co., 1978.

Stanislavski, Constantin. *An Actor Prepares*. New York: Theater Arts Books, 1972.

Triplett, Robert. *Stagefright*. Chicago: Nelson-Hall, 1984.

Watkins, Dwight Everett, A.M. and Harrison M. Karr, Ph.D. *Stage Fright and What To Do About It*. Boston, MA: Expression Company, 1940.

Yoga & Body Work

Ajaya, Swami. *Yoga Psychology, A Practice Guide to Meditation*. Honesdale, PA: Himalayan International Institute of Yoga Science and Philosophy, 1976.

Arya, Pandit Usharbudh, D.Litt.. *Philosophy of Hatha Yoga*. Honesdale, PA: Himalayan International Institute of Yoga Science and Philosophy, 1985.

Dychtwald, Ken. *Bodymind*. Los Angeles: Jeremy P. Tarcher, Inc., 1986.

Feitis, Rosemary, Ed. *Ida Rolf Talks About Rolfing and Physical Reality*. New York: Harper & Row, 1978.

Leboyer, Frederick. *The Art of Breathing*. Munich: Kosel Verlag GmbH & Co., 1985.

Rama, Swami, Rudolph Ballentine, M.D., and Alan Hymes, M.D. *Science of Breath, A Practical Guide*. Honesdale, PA: Himalayan International Institute of Yoga Science and Philosophy, 1979.

Alexander Technique

Barker, Sarah. *The Alexander Technique: The Revolutionary Way To Use Your Body For Total Energy.* New York: Bantam Books, 1978.

Cohen-Nehemia, M. *The Mitzvah Exercise and Its Principle.* Toronto: The Canadian Centre for the Alexander Technique, 1983.

Jones, Frank Pierce. *The Alexander Technique--Body Awareness in Action.* New York: Schocken Books, 1976.

Stransky, Judith with Robert B. Stone, Ph.D.. *The Alexander Technique: Joy In The Life of Your Body.* New York: Beaufort Books, Inc., 1981.

Body Language

Kurtz, Ron and Hector Prestera, M.D. *The Body Reveals.* New York: Harper & Row/Quicksilver Books, 1976.

Self Help

Bates, Charles T. *Ransoming The Mind: An Integration of Yoga and Modern Therapy.* St. Paul, Minn.: YES International Publishers, 1986.

Butterworth, Eric. *Discover the Power Within You, A Guide to the Unexplored Depths Within, Based on the Actual Teachings of Jesus.* New York: Harper & Row, 1968.

Gawain, Shakti. *Living in the Light.* Mill Valley, CA: Whatever Publishing, Inc., 1986.

Holmes, Ernest. *The Science of Mind.* New York: Dodd, Mead & Co., 1938.

Hornaday, William H.D. and Harlan Ware, Dodd. *The Inner Light: An Informal Portrait of a Philosopher.* New York: Mead & Co., 1964.

Peale, Norman Vincent. *The Power of Positive Thinking.* New York: Prentice Hall, 1952.

Vargas, Marjorie Fink. *Louder Than Words.* Ames, Iowa: Iowa State University Press, 1986.

Public Speaking

Doolittle, Robert J. *Professionally Speaking*. Glenview, IL: Scott, Foresman and Company, 1984.

Faludi, Susan. "Speak For Yourself." *The New York Times*, Feb. 3, 1992.

Frady, Marshall. Profiles (Jesse Jackson—Part I). *The New Yorker*, Feb. 3, 1992.

Rogers, Natalie H. *How To Speak Without Fear: Talk-Power*. New York: Dodd, Mead & Co., 1982.

Visualization

Gawain, Shakti. *Creative Visualization*. Toronto: Bantam Books, 1979.

Kekule Memorial Lecture, *J. Chem. Soc.*, 73, 100 (1898).

Samuels, Mike, M.D., and Nancy Samuels. *Seeing With The Mind's Eye—The History, Techniques and Uses of Visualization*. New York: Random House, 1975.

Neurolinguistic Programming

Bandler, Richard and John Grinder. *Frogs Into Princes*. Moab, Utah: Real People Press, 1979.

Bandler, Richard and John Grinder. *Reframing*. Moab, Utah: Real People Press, 1982.

Bandler, Richard; Edited by Steve Andreas and Connirae Andreas. *Using Your Brain—For A Change*. Moab, Utah: Real People Press, 1985.

Grinder, John and Richard Bandler; edited by Connirae Andreas. *Trance-Formations: Neurolinguistic Programming and The Structure of Hypnosis*. Moab, Utah: Real People Press, 1981.

Laborde, Genie. *Influencing With Integrity*. Mountain View, CA: Syntony Publishing, 1984.

Index

About The Author

Mary Stark is a professional actress and a member of the Antaeus Repertory Company at the Mark Taper Forum. She is also a writer, a director, and a singer with the Los Angeles Master Chorale.

Mary teaches Scene Study for Actors and The Professional ACT workshops. She graduated from Earlham College and studied acting at the Hedgerow Theatre School in Moylan, Pennsylvania, at the Lion Theatre Company in New York, and with John Franklyn-Robbins and Tom McNally.

She created her own one-woman show, *White Ashes: The Life and Writings of Harriet Beecher Stowe,* and has performed it at the Beecher Family Reunion, the Smithsonian Institution, and colleges, universities, women's groups, and churches across the country. It is a featured presentation of the Pacific Mountain Network's *Classroom Channel* and the Los Angeles cable series, *Playhouse 1990's.*

She has directed *Come Back to the Five & Dime, Jimmy Dean, Jimmy Dean* (Blackfriars in Rochester), *Working, How To Succeed in Business Without Really Trying,* and *Merrily We Roll Along* (Rochester Institute of Technology).

Her acting credits include Griselda and Win in *Top Girls,* the Reasonable Woman in *The Trojan Women,* Hesione in *Heartbreak House,* and Lady Plyant in *The Double Dealer* (Antaeus Company). She played Emily Dickinson opposite her husband, Frank Dwyer, playing Walt Whitman, in *I'm Nobody . . . Who Are You?* for Jerome Lawrence's Master of Professional Writing Seminar at USC. Among other roles, Mary played Helen in *Born Yesterday* (California Theatre of Performing Art), Miss Yorke in *The Rose Tattoo,* Mrs. Krebs in *Inherit The Wind,* Mrs. Cratchit in *A Christmas Carol* (Rochester, New York's GeVa Theatre), Sally in *Talley's Folly,* Twirler in *Talking With . . .,* and June in *The Fifth of July* (University of Rochester Summer Theatre).

Presentation Self Assessment

1) What did I communicate through my body language? Did my posture present the image I desired? Were my gestures natural and effortless?

2) Did I establish and maintain eye-contact with the audience?

3) Was my body prepared for the presentation by a program of physical exercise and balanced eating?

4) Before my presentation, did I clearly define my intention or objective?

5) Did I focus on a Point of Concentration (breath or something else)?

6) Before the presentation, did I warm up my voice and body and calm my mind through my personal method of focusing?

7) Did I allow imagination and playfulness to enhance my expressiveness?

8) Did I use listening skills to create rapport with the audience? Did I research my audience's personal history to find common motivators and dovetail my objectives to their goals?

9) Did I supplement my preparation with visualizations and verbal affirmations for success?

10) Did I investigate any feelings of stagefright and re-program that response as excitement, as fuel for my presentation?

11) Did I view the audience as my ally, as the people who are helping me to develop my skills as a confident and expressive communicator?

For any question to which you answered "no," read:

1) .... Chapter 2

2) .... Chapter 2

3) .... Chapter 3

4) .... Chapter 4

5) .... Chapter 4

6) .... Chapter 5

7) .... Chapter 5

8) .... Chapter 6

9) .... Chapter 6

10) .... Chapter 7

11) .... Chapter 7

METAMORPHOUS PRESS

Metamorphous Press is a publisher of books and other media providing resources for personal growth and positive change. MP publishes leading-edge ideas that help people strengthen their unique talents and discover that we are responsible for our own realities. Many of our titles center around Neurolinguistic Programming (NLP). NLP is an exciting, practical, and powerful model of observable patterns of behavior and communication and the processes that underlie them.

Metamorphous Press provides selections in many useful subject areas such as communication, health and fitness, education, business and sales, therapy, selections for young persons, and other subjects of general and specific interest. Our products are available in fine bookstores around the world.

Our distributors for North America are:

Baker & Taylor
Bookpeople
Ingram
Inland Book Co.
Metamorphous
Advanced Product Services
Moving Books, Inc.
New Leaf
Pacific Pipeline
The Distributors

For those of you overseas, we are distributed by:

Airlift (UK, Western Europe)
Specialist Publications (Australia)

New selections are added regularly and availability and prices change, so ask for a current catalog or to be put on our mailing list. If you have difficulty finding our products in your favorite store, or if you prefer to order by mail, we will be happy to make our books and other products available to you directly. Your involvement and interest in what we do is always welcome. Please write or call us at:

Metamorphous Press
P.O. Box 10616
Portland, OR 97210
(503) 228-4972

TOLL FREE ORDERING
1-800-937-7771